THE PSYCHOLOGY OF YOUR POWERFUL UNCONCIOUS MIND

GURU PRASAD SWAIN

Made with ♥ on the Notion Press Platform
www.notionpress.com

Summery-

The mind and its phenomena of qualia and consciousness are non-material entities with information and information processing as their essence. They evolved into existence to help increase the survival chance of the species that possess them. Why do we have the mind, qualia, and consciousness as they are manifesting phenomenally as vision, sound, smell, emotion, thought, etc. that we can experience mentally why are we not like computers or robots, doing everything "in the dark", without those phenomenal manifestations occurring? The answer is because the mind, qualia, and consciousness that manifest phenomenally have additional physical effects from their phenomenal manifestations, and those effects help increase the survival chance of ourselves and our species. Therefore, the mind, qualia, and consciousness as they are – having phenomenal manifestations – evolved into existence to help us and our species survive better. How do those phenomenal manifestations, the seemingly non-physical manifestations – such as the vision of the red colour, the musical sound, and the happy emotion in our mind, occur from neural processes, which are just physical processes – how can physical processes give rise to those seemingly non-physical phenomenal manifestations? ... The answer is because some neural processes have neural signals that mean, in the neural language, phenomenal manifestations, when these signals are read in the neural system, they will be interpreted as phenomenal manifestations, and phenomenal manifestations naturally and inevitably occur in the neural system. This is how qualia and consciousness occur with all their phenomenal manifestations in the physical brain.

Quick proof $\Rightarrow$ Qualia have physical effect

Quick proof $\Rightarrow$ Qualia are neural signals

"The Basic Theory of the Mind" is a physical theory about the mind and its phenomena, such as qualia and consciousness. It also involves related matters including the hard problem of consciousness, the explanatory gap, variable qualia, p-zombies, and free will. This theory is a scientifically verifiable theory – it is based on physical evidence and provides experimentally testable predictions.

The Mind-

The mind is one thing that has always fascinated and puzzled us. It is the only thing that we can be certain of existing, yet, apparently, we do not know exactly what it is, how it occurs, and why it occurs. This is in contrast to things outside the mind, such as houses, cars, and even other people, which we cannot be certain that they really exist – they may be just illusions – yet, apparently, we know what they are, how they occur, and why they occur. What is more, the phenomena of qualia and consciousness, such as the red colour as it appears phenomenally red in our mind and our phenomenal conscious awareness and experience of that red colour, have always been baffling – what is their nature, how and why do they occur, and cannot there be just the mind without them? Fortunately, with centuries of studying these matters, first by philosophers and later also by neurologists, neuroscientists, and other scientists in related fields, we now have a wealth of scientific evidence and concepts that are complete enough to form a theory that can answer these great puzzles. The Basic Theory of the Mind -

Based on the wealth of scientific evidence and concepts, this theory has been formed. Its essence is as follows:

1. From the physical properties of the mind and those of the brain (the alive, processing brain), it can be concluded that the mind always occurs, exists, and functions with the brain and that the brain always occurs, exists, and functions with the mind. Both never occur alone without the other. They are a unity. Each is the intrinsic, equivalent, but different (non-material vs material) aspect of this unity.

2. From the physical properties of the mind and those of the brain's information-processing processes, which are non-material processes, it can be concluded that the mind is the composite of the information-processing processes of the brain "What happens when we see, hear, and smell things around us, experience moods, think of various things, plan appropriate actions, and command our hands, lips, and body to move, if not information, information, and information are being processed. We are just informational entities, ever processing information and living on the informational side of the universe."

1. The mind is an information-processing entity. Because the mind is a composite of information-processing processes, it is an informational entity – a non-material entity that is composed of information and information processing, and because the information processing processes that form the mind are innumerable in number and involve information that ranges from simple to very advanced, the mind is an informational entity in a highly advanced form. And, because the mind is a non-material, informational entity, it is not a conventional physical entity (or mechanical entity) like mass, energy, or force; that is why it is so different from the conventional physical entities.

3. Qualia, the mental phenomena that appear phenomenally in our mind and that we can consciously experience, such as the vision of a house, the sound of a song, and the door of a rose in our mind, are physical phenomena. They are governed by physical laws and are physically predictable. 2. Qualia are mental phenomena that we can consciously experience in our mind.

Specifically, they are neural process associated physical phenomena.

[Quick proof ⇒ Qualia are physical phenomena]

4. From the physical properties of qualia and those of special kinds of neural-process signalling pattern, which are neural information and non-material, it can be concluded that qualia are special kinds of neural-process signalling pattern.

"If we look around and consciously experience the visual qualia occurring right in front of us now, with the facts that our consciousness can experience the visual qualia and that the only things the consciousness neural process is capable of reading are signalling patterns of neural processes, it is inescapable to conclude that we are, in fact, experiencing the signalling patterns of neural processes!"

[Quick proof ⇒ Qualia are signalling patterns]

Because neural-process signalling patterns are neural information, qualia are special kinds of neural information — neural information in specialized forms that, when read by neural processes, are interpreted to be entities with phenomenal appearances or qualia that appear phenomenally in our mind signalling pattern and qualia and consciousness

3. When read by neural processes, a normal signalling pattern (A) for a visual perception of a house means "House", so the mind gets only the physical information of the house (such as its width, length, height, luminosity, and colours) but not the information of what the house looks like. But a special signalling pattern (B) for a visual perception of the same house means "House and what the house looks like"; consequently, a quale of the house naturally and inevitably occurs in the mind. Like the mind, qualia are non-material, informational entities, not mechanical entities. And this answers the hard problem of qualia and bridges the explanatory gap of how non-material phenomenal qualia can arise from material neural processes: non-material phenomenal qualia are neural signalling patterns, which always exist intrinsically in material neural processes — no novel, non-material entities arise or emerge from material

neural processes to be qualia.

5. From the physical properties of consciousness and those of a special kind of re-entrant signalling state, which is the neural information of the consciousness neural process and is non-material, it can be concluded that consciousness is a special kind of re-entrant signalling state. Because a neural-process signalling state is neural information consciousness is a special kind of neural information – neural information in a specialized form that, when read by the consciousness neural process itself by the process of re-entrant signalling, is interpreted to be entities with phenomenal appearances or consciousness that appears phenomenally in our mind signalling state and consciousness

4. When read by the consciousness neural process by the process of re-entrant signalling, a special signalling state of a visual perception of a house means "conscious awareness and experience of what the house looks like"; consequently, phenomenal consciousness of the house naturally and inevitably occurs. Like the mind and qualia, consciousness is a non-material, informational entity, not a mechanical entity. And this answers the hard problem of consciousness and bridges the explanatory gap of how non-material phenomenal consciousness can arise from the material consciousness neural process: non-material phenomenal consciousness is a signalling state that always exists intrinsically in the material consciousness neural process – no novel, non-material entity arises or emerges from the material consciousness neural process to be consciousness.

6. The fact that qualia and conscious awareness and conscious experiences of the qualia occur in only the final-stage sensory perception neural processes and the highest-level cognitive and executive neural processes, which are the latest-evolved neural processes, and never occur in the more primitive neural processes, such as the brainstem, cerebellum, and basal ganglia, or over the whole brain scattered, indicates that they are not randomly occurring phenomena but are evolved functions of the nervous system.

7. Because a neural process that performs a certain function (such as perceiving a vision) without qualia occurring and a neural process that performs that same function (such as perceiving a vision) with qualia occurring have different information in the processes, they have different signalling patterns (to convey different information). Therefore, they have different physical effects on other neural processes, at least from the different effects of different signalling patterns. Qualia thus have physical effects. signalling patterns Ans meanings

5. Different signalling patterns have different meanings and different effects Also, because we do have conscious awareness and conscious experiences of qualia, qualia must certainly induce the consciousness neural process to function to be consciously aware of and to consciously experience the qualia; therefore, because the consciousness neural process is a physical process, qualia cause changes in a physical process and thus have physical effects. Similarly, it can be concluded that consciousness (conscious awareness and conscious experiences) has physical effects. Therefore, qualia and consciousness are evolved neural functions that have physical effects.

8. Because a function requires resources in building, maintaining, and operating the function and may have some negative effects, if its overall effects do not help increase the survival chance of the animals that have the function, those animals and the function will likely become extinct in the evolutionary process. This is especially true for a major function in a critical organ as in the case of qualia and consciousness in the brain. The fact that qualia and consciousness still exist today indicates that they have been selected to remain in the evolutionary process. This means that their overall effects must help increase the survival chance of the species that have them. Qualia and consciousness, in the form that they are – phenomenal qualia and phenomenal consciousness, or qualia and consciousness that appear phenomenally in our mind – thus are evolved functions to help increase the survival chance of the species, including humans, that have them. This is the scientific answer to the other part of the hard problem of consciousness: why does consciousness in the form of phenomenal consciousness occur in this universe? This is also the scientific answer to one of the most basic questions of our lives: why do "we" exist? In conclusion:

"We" – our mind, qualia, and consciousness – exist

to increase the survival chance of ourselves

... and our species.

"You" – your mind, qualia, and consciousness – exist

to increase the survival chance of yourself

... and your species.

Green Mind Theory: How Brain-Body-Behaviour Links into Natural and Social Environments for Healthy Habits by Jules Pretty 1 Orchidometer Rogerson 2, ORCID and Barton ORCID

School of Biological Sciences, University of Essex, Colchester CO4 3SQ, UK school of Sport, Rehabilitation and Exercise Sciences, University of Essex, Colchester CO4 3SQ, UK

Author to whom correspondence should be addressed. All authors contributed equally to this work. Int. J. Environ. Res. Public Health 2017, 14(7), 706.

We propose a Green Mind Theory (GMT) to link the human mind with the brain and body and connect the body into natural and social environments. The processes are reciprocal: environments shape bodies, brains, and minds; minds change body behaviours that shape the external environment. GMT offers routes to improved individual well-being whilst building towards greener economies. It builds upon research on green exercise and nature-based therapies and draws on understanding derived from neuroscience and brain plasticity, spiritual and wisdom traditions, the lifeways of original cultures, and material consumption behaviours. We set out a simple metaphor for brain function: a bottom brain stem that is fast-acting, involuntary, impulsive, and the driver of fight and flight behaviours; a top brain cortex that is slower, voluntary, the centre for learning, and the driver of rest and digest. The bottom brain reacts before thought and directs the sympathetic nervous system. The top brain is calming, directing the parasympathetic nervous system. Here, we call the top brain blue and the bottom brain red; too much red brain is bad for health. In modern high-consumption economies, life has often come to be lived on red alert. An over-active red mode impacts the gastrointestinal, immune, cardiovascular, and endocrine systems. We develop our knowledge of nature-based interventions and suggest a framework for the blue brain-red brain-green mind. We show how activities involving immersive-attention quieten internal chatter, how habits affect behaviours across the life course, how long habits take to be formed and hard-wired into daily practice, the role of place making, and finally how green minds could foster prosocial and greener economies. We conclude with observations on twelve research priorities and health interventions, and ten calls to action.

Keywords: green minds; green exercise; nature and health; healthy behaviours

1. Recent Findings from Research on Nature and Health We have undertaken over a decade of research into the contexts, effects, and outcomes of green exercise and nature-based interventions, showing in a wide variety of contexts that physical activity in the presence of nature improves health and well-being We have found no groups who have not benefitted: all

ages, genders, ethnicities, and social classes respond positively to green exercise. We have shown that all-natural environments are beneficial: from urban parks to biodiversity-rich ones, from small local to large landscapes, and from domesticated gardens to the farmed and wild. We coined the phrase dose of nature to articulate that exposure to green exercise is analogous to a medical dose to the body, improving mental health We have shown that the deliberate therapeutic use of natural environments (e.g., gardens, allotments, care farms, and wild places) has both short and long term positive effects on groups under mental stress, including at-risk children and youth, refugees, probationers, dementia sufferers, office workers, and mental health patients. The natural environment is now understood to provide vital health services as well as other environmental services These health services include direct and indirect effects on physical and mental health, and reductions in the threats of pollution and disease vectors.

Further research has filled many gaps, exploring inner mechanisms, external social processes, interactions with place and behaviours across the life course. It has been shown that greener environments reducing social inequality and having particularly positive impacts on mental well-being, that physical labour in the home is important for health and longevity and that blue space (locations in sight of water) is as important as green: it is not the colour that matters, but the opportunity to behave in a way that improves well-being. A meta-analysis of nature connectivity and well-being has shown the more connected to nature a person is, the greater is their life satisfaction. At the same time, the design of human settlements and buildings influences human health suggesting that natural places can be thought of as healing places Typical urban settings are more discomforting, with metabolic and well-being consequences. Exposure to nature reduces internal stress markers and produces healthier cortisol profiles. Knowing is important too. knowledge of being treated (both dose of nature and drug medication) causes a release of endogenous opioids that are non-addictive: the placebo effect demonstrates the mechanisms for self-healing (of some conditions) Life course and longitudinal studies (e.g., Caerphilly men, Dunedin, Maudsley and Cambridge cohorts, Milwaukee nuns, Harvard alumni) have shown how choices on behaviours, consumption, and mental states directly affect health and well-being over many decades. These studies demonstrate the value of early interventions with children whose cognitive outcomes are improved when regularly exposed to activity in natural places (playgrounds, gardens, and woodlands).

We have calculated the annual health costs of seven lifestyle-related conditions in the U.K. (obesity, type 2 diabetes, loneliness, cardiovascular diseases, mental ill-health, dementias, and physical inactivity), all of which are influenced by a lack of physical activity, links to natural places, and links to community and people; annually these amount to around £180 billion. All these conditions are influenced by a lack of physical activity, links to natural places, and links to community and people, with annual health costs ranging from £8–105 billion (Table 1). This suggests that high levels of material consumption in affluent countries have not necessarily brought increased health and well-being for all; that consumption patterns in most countries of the world are converging on those typical to the affluent; and that new ways of living are required that emphasise non-material consumption if planetary and personal harm is to be avoided

Table 1. The annual costs of the health externalities arising from modern lifestyles, U.K.

Table

Many of the drivers of ill-health in Table 1 are behaviour- and lifestyle-related: too many calories consumed in food and drink, too little physical activity, and too little social engagement. Through a variety of interventions, there is now the prospect of the U.K. becoming virtually tobacco-free (<16% of the adult population now smoke tobacco, down from 50% in the mid-1970s). Yet the implementation of healthy food, activity, and engagement activities for whole populations seems impossible, despite advances on nudge tactics (a concept that involves positive reinforcement to achieve non-forced compliance) Social and economic environments do shape behaviours. Residents of London walk 292 miles per year; but rural people walk just 122 miles. Obesity afflicts 35% of adults in the U.S.; in Manhattan, where there are pavements and public transport, people walk more, and only 15% are obese. In the Japanese, Sardinian, and Costa Rican longevity hotspots, cultures encourage healthy and tasty foods, regular physical activity outdoors, social connections, and continued cognitive engagement. Individual choices do not arise from failures of free-will but are shaped by the interactions between the design of lived environments, transport systems, institutional inertia, advertising and corporate self-interest, and access to green space. Here, we explore how behaviours benefitting health can be adopted and encouraged. 2. Red Brain, Blue Brain, Green Mind

We are proposing a Green Mind Theory (GMT) that links the human mind with the brain and body and connects the body with natural and social environments. The processes are reciprocal: environments shape bodies, brains, and minds; minds change body behaviours that shape social interactions and natural capital. GMT offers opportunities for improving individual well-being whilst building towards greener and prosocial economies that could protect the planetary future. The empirical understanding of green minds derives from evidence on neuroscience and brain plasticity, from spiritual and wisdom traditions from mindfulness-related and talking therapies from green exercise activities in nature from the lifeways of indigenous groups and from material consumption behaviours and the potential emergence of green and prosocial economies

We outline how and why pathways of poor health can be engaged by surrounding natural and social environments in ways that promote reciprocal individual-society-natural well-being. Our concern is not to assume a comprehensive description of many complex brain-body interactions, nor to take a simple behaviourist model whereby well-being or happiness can appear to be guaranteed. Our desire is to use an emerging understanding of brain-body-behaviours to develop pathways and interventions for better health and well-being.

We propose a simple brain metaphor with levels representing different stages of mammal-hominid evolution The brain stem (bottom brain) is the oldest and contains survival functions: it is fast responding, involuntary, automatic, impulsive, driven by emotions, and is the executor for habits and routines. In the mid-brain, the limbic/sub-cortex system is the central region comprising the hippocampus, hypothalamus and thalamus, and amygdala: it is the centre for emotions, memory forming, and bonding. The top-brain cortex is the most recent, having expanded in size rapidly during the later stages of hominid evolution: it is slower, voluntary, able to learn and plan, make internal choices, and contains centres for the social abilities of empathy and language. The top brain is calming, drives the parasympathetic nervous system (PNS), and is characterised by rest-and-digest. The bottom brain is spiked into action by the amygdala, the sentinel for emotional meaning, which drives the sympathetic nervous system (SNS) via the hypothalamus pituitary adrenal axis (HPAA) and is characterised by fight-and-flight. We call the top brain blue, and the bottom brain red.

We use the term green mind to suggest an optimal mixed mode of mainly activated PNS, interest and excitement associated mild SNS stimulation, and the presence of only occasional SNS spikes for alarm response. A mix of blue and red is best for health and well-being. Too much red brain is detrimental for health. The key endogenous neurotransmitters, hormones, and peptide pathways are serotonin (key to sleep and mood); dopamine (aids approach, attention, and rewards, but when it falls it makes us feel unpleasant); norepinephrine (promotes alertness and arousal); acetylcholine (promotes wakefulness and learning); opioids (reduces pain and buffer stress); oxytocin (a key role in bonding and feelings of bliss); cortisol (stimulates amygdala and inhibits hippocampus); oestrogen (key in memory); and adrenalin (stress hormone). Our proposal for the greener mind centres on activities that bring immersion-attentiveness, so calming the mind. We will later show how these centres on the choice architecture for engagements with nature, with other people, and with craft-skill based activities. Green Mind Theory suggests that desirable fundamentals to well-being are in reach of everyone. Yet the negativity bias of the brain has become dominant in modern living. A summary of the key differences between the modern and green mind is shown in Table 2.

Table 2. Ten differences between mind typical of modern affluent culture and the green mind.

Table

3. The Brain's Negativity Bias and Causes of Suffering

It is plausible that natural selection has built a negativity bias into the brain-mind the amygdala responds immediately to alerts and succeeds by being over-responsive. In evolutionary history, to miss one threat meant death; to miss one positive signal was not necessarily critical. The brain-mind thus evolved fast-acting and over-responsive fight-flight as the default mode. There is no moderation to the amygdala. It is a binary responder: fully on or off and responding before thought. In hunter-gatherer-cultivator communities (the old economies: sites for millions of years of prior evolution, the blue brain mode tends to dominate the predator or poisonous snake was rare, threats from other hominid bands also scarce. By contrast, in modern affluent cultures dominated by material consumption and dashed hope, the red alert mode is regularly activated. Modern life appears to be lived on simmer reducing almost non-stop SNS-HPAA activation.

Repeated SNS-HPAA stimulation leads to an over-reactive amygdala, resulting in high anxiety and the continual shading of memories with fear and anxiety. The current world gradually looks and feels worse, as does the past. The hippocampus is worn down, and memories harder to retain. Cortisol further suppresses new neurons in the hippocampus. Too much SNS-HPAA has negative impacts on the gastrointestinal system (more ulcers, inflammatory bowel syndrome), on the immune system (more colds and flu, slower wound healing), on the cardiovascular system (hardened arteries), and on the endocrine system (producing type 2 diabetes) Stress manifested as conditions (e.g., post-traumatic stress disorder (PTSD), depression) and illness (e.g., cardio-vascular disease) manifests internally as accumulation over long time periods of gradually worsening internal responses to the same stressors. Over time, continuing red brain activity exacts a cost, accelerating disease mechanisms, especially CVD, and the atrophy of brain structures (especially the hippocampus). Repeated hits of stress can leave stress hormone levels continually high, with no recovery period.

Modern living is often characterised by cognitive overload, impulsive habits, and individual behaviours that have led to a new generation of health challenges Just as shortages of food—eras of never-quite-enough—were solved in the 1950s–1970s in affluent countries, so food over-consumption became a leading problem just as eras of challenging transport requiring high energy expenditure ended, so inactivity and sedentary behaviours became common health problems. With these have come increased anxiety, guilt, and stress in a cosy modern world, many have forgotten discomfort finding it easy to habituate over-eating or drinking, or a reliance on pharmaceutical interventions. In time, the habits evolve into pre-emptive strikes: promoting consumption before the anticipated discomfort. Some spiritual and wisdom traditions call the red alerts first arrows these are fired by the amygdala and cannot be avoided. The second arrows, comprising how we feel in response to the first, commonly result in feelings of unfairness, guilt, further fear, anger, upset, and anxiety. Sometimes second arrows arise from anxious expectation, even when there have been no first arrow Threat signals are effective precisely because they are unpleasant. They should be they make us suffer.

The first arrow threat alarm causes the amygdala to stimulate the thalamus, which sends norepinephrine to the brain stem (red brain). The SNS signals organs and muscles to ready for fight-flight, the hypothalamus now signalling the pituitary to instruct the adrenal glands to release adrenaline, cortisol, and epinephrine. The body is now on red alert, the epinephrine having increased heart rate and dilated pupils for more light, the cortisol suppressing the immune system and hippocampus. The executive control of the prefrontal cortex is switched off. Suffering arising from first arrows is thus embodied and works through the cascade of SNS and HPAA. Most of the time, we hardly notice this is happening.

Modern affluent countries contain lonelier people and have a growing number of adults living alone Lonely adults display elevated cortisol and epinephrine levels and have higher blood pressure; the more active SNS-HPAA results in poorer sleep and lower immune function; it accelerates physiological decline with age Further linking the brain with behaviour, individuals with smaller social networks tend to have a smaller amygdala and hippocampus: structures that play an important role in social behaviour The lonely are red brain dominant, and their lifespan is reduced. In modern living, first arrows have become more common, and together with second arrows have negative impacts on memory, general well-being, and habit forming. A strong blue brain can dampen second arrows.

4. Immersion and Attentiveness to Quiet the Chatter A green mind should have a healthy mix of brain states, with a predominance of calm blue. A range of different descriptors have been used to describe a state of mind that results in a temporary dampening of second arrows by building up the PNS: focus, attention, awareness, and immersion. There is clear evidence to show that activities that are immersive and involve focused attention are effective in improving well-being they cause instant physiological changes by reducing oxygen consumption, lowering heart rate and blood pressure, and increasing the release of serotonin and dopamine The importance of recovering the capacity to focus attention was first proposed by Kaplan and Kaplan leading to a growing understanding of the restorative benefits of nature A variety of stressors cause attention fatigue: Attention Restoration Theory showed how focused attention, with positive well-being outcomes, could be recovered or restored by engagement with a variety of environments, both natural and non-natural More recently, research on palatogenesis, the range of factors supporting health and well-being, has developed an understanding of how environments can both deplete and restore internal resources here, we suggest it is the immersion and activation of the PNS that is the key mechanism. Some environments are thus seen as restorative, as are some behaviours and activities. We know that immersive-attention is an element of some green exercise, arising during walking, moderate running, and gardening during meditative activities such as yoga, tai chi, and mindfulness and during many craft and skill-based activities such as woodwork, painting, knitting, and needlework In some, exercise involves no more than sitting; in others, it is part of cultural events: community dancing and singing of sinning of Tibet, the haka of Māori in New Zealand, the chain dance of Faroe, the reamer of Iceland, the shadow puppetry of Indonesia, the ceremonial dances of American Indian tribes, and forest bathing in Japan Being highly attentive could have brought evolutionary advantage to hunter-gatherer-cultivators. Watchful awareness is central to the hunt; is vital for caring for plants and animals across the seasons; is critical to memory creation for sources of water and signals for weather events. Hunter-gatherer-cultivators spent large amounts of time waiting, observing keenly, and preparing and eating food. Yet in material cultures and economies where a life on automatic seems a modern malaise, millions actively choose opportunities for quiet and calm: watching sunsets, beach holidays, being with friends, and activities that require focus and take time to learn. A second feature of a brain dominated by second arrows is the endless chatter that originates in the verbal and language centres of the left prefrontal cortex. This chatter comprises the loops of internal voice that act as commentary on past events, future possibilities, and current concerns the autobiographical self runs loops of past and future and is often self-critical. Anxiety retunes memories of the past, gradually making them feel worse. Immersive-attentive activities are calming and take time. They activate the PNS, and increase

neurone growth in the insula, hippocampus, and prefrontal cortex, particularly the left prefrontal cortex (PFC) where feelings of well-being reside. A steady release of dopamine is produced, increasing a sense of well-being. The PNS further decreases cortisol and strengthens the activity of the immune system. Immersive attentiveness can thus feel like a high vantage point, being on a hill looking down on the distant valley below, or on cliffs looking at the silent sea. When the green mind is quiet, the self is stilled. A wandering mind is an unhappy mind

5. Habits and Behaviours in the Life course

Planning and learning occur in the PFC, and as routines are automated so they are sent downwards to the mid and lower brains and tend to remain fixed unless brought back up for specific improvements. As we habituate a routine more, so the basal ganglia take over from the PFC and automate the routine, allowing us to pay less attention (and use up less energy). This occurs in the learning of language, the gait of walking, the poise of sitting, preferences for foods, and the mode of driving a car or riding a bicycle. All require hours of practice, but once learned no longer require active attention. Many of the modern conditions of ill-health result from behaviours gradually adopted over time and are thus hard to challenge, including eating and drinking habits, smoking, sedentary lifestyles, reduced direct contacts with family and community, less active transport, reduced contact with green places, and increased use of pharmaceutical solutions to ill-health Will-power and focus are vital capabilities for learning skill-based habits. To learn a language (the first or more), arithmetic and times tables, to drive a vehicle, all require practice. The greater the cognitive control by the PFC, the less anxiety we suffer. In the Dunedin longitudinal study, children with the greatest willpower early in life had the best health outcomes during the life course. The critical years for children to learn self-control are 5–8 years of age: if they do, this improves cognitive capability Time outdoors as a child facilitates, and predicts, adult health

One enduring heuristic suggests it takes ten thousand hours to learn to become an expert Yet for most behaviours it is far fewer, as repetition sooner sends routines to the bottom brain. Repeated behaviours in consistent settings proceed more efficiently and are strengthened through association between situation (environmental cues) and action Experimental research has shown it takes 28 to 84 days to form a habit, depending on time spent per day, or ten weeks for healthy habits to become fixed Thirty minutes a day for 30 days of time in nature has been shown to improve well-being, mood, and mindfulness, though for this to become fixed as a habit, it is likely to need three times the number of days for long-term adherence

Weekly interventions of walking and tai chi for 40 and 52 weeks have been shown to increase hippocampus volume in the elderly We thus suggest a rule of thumb of 50 days at one hour per day, or 100 days (approximately 3 months) at half an hour per day, to produce changes in the brain and result in fixes to behaviour. To improve or change a habituated routine, it needs to be brought back to the PFC, evaluated, and amended. But changing ingrained habits is hard: we must force the body to do something different as it will not choose voluntarily to do so. Habits must be brought back up to the blue brain and become subject to specific attention. In the increasingly typical modern life course, many people also give up activities that brought them pleasure on the grounds that they have neither the time nor the energy to continue. Over the life course, inch by inch, we cede territory to automated behaviours and habits that often bring discontent. We pay less attention to eating well, forget friends, and become less active. Halpern posed a question: when did you stop dancing? One significant policy and practice challenge is to identify the habit-releasers for improved health: new behaviours need forceful and sometimes fierce action. Other centres on the choice architecture of social and cultural environments that in turn shape choices about behaviours The U.K.'s Behavioural Insight Team, or Nudge Unit, has demonstrated how small nudges can lead to shifts in behaviours across large populations. But frequent practice is still required to fix new patterns in the brain: the fifty hours. The key concept is that the brain changes because of body behaviours: the property of neuroplasticity

6. Neuroplasticity and Placebos Neuroplasticity is the property of the brain to change structure and function by responding to actions by the body, to signals received from the external world, and to mental experiences. In this way, external and internal signals are not materially different: they are just signals. It is also understood that neurons that fire together, wire together; and those not used will die back. The conventional predominant view of the brain-mind is that if it breaks down, nothing can be done. The concept of neuroplasticity suggests new opportunities for directed or chosen changes across the life course. The first example centres on pain and pain control. Acute pain is a signal to attend to a problem immediately. But neuropathic-chronic pain is different: it comprises the incessant false alarms of the afterlife of acute pain. These repeated mental experiences cause structural changes in the brain, and the pain map continues expanding, and invading parts of the brain that process thought, sensations, images, and memory Persistent and chronic pain is also demoralising setting off new red alerts from the amygdala. An understanding of neuroplasticity has shown that the pain gate can be raised by endorphins, and these can be released by immersion-attentiveness activities such as mindfulness, meditation, and tai chi The gate rises, the pain sensations fall, and counter-stimulations in the invaded parts of the brain push away the pain

memories. However, individuals must be relentless in forming this new habit: they must be more relentless than the pain that produced the map The placebo effect (PE) is a second example and is no less real because it is driven by thought. It causes as many changes in the brain as does medication. The placebo has long been conceptualised as an inert process, and thus used as an experimental control for drug testing. But recent research on the PE has shown the potential benefits of self-healing. The PE is a genuine phenomenon driven by expectancy in both patient and physicians/nurses, and has yielded beneficial clinical results for angina, bronchial asthma, herpes, ulcers, inflammatory bowel syndrome, and persistent pain The PE mechanism centres on the self-release of non-addictive endogenous opioids. It has been noted that alternative therapies with no clear scientific explanation but with elaborate rituals and beliefs can thus induce placebo effects, particularly if there is a good personal relationship between the practitioner and the patient It has also been shown that treatment augmented with warmth, attention, and confidence improves clinical outcomes. Patients thus engage in treating themselves if physicians, nurses, and carers have a friendly manner, engage in active listening, show empathy, allow periods of silence in conversation, and communicate confidence and positive expectations The British Medical Association has reinforced the importance of compassion and empathy for patient-centred care. In noting the high levels of boredom on hospital wards, where there is too little physical activity, they have recommended hospitals engage in deliberate social activities, such as creative writing, music, visual art, dance, and singing. Better design would help too, including for creating healing gardens

7. Place Making

The green mind suggests that individuals link to natural places that are recognisable and individualised. These might include urban parks, gardens, nature reserves, and walking routes (including for dog walkers). In the contemporary affluent world, chronic place lessness has become endemic. People spend less time outdoors, travel less by walking and cycling, and move to a new house more often Children's disconnection from natural places stores up future problems, as fewer memories are made of life events in the critical middle age of childhood from 5 to 11 years The structure of physical and natural environments is now well-established as having an impact on physical and mental health with physical activity in cities by cycling and walking reducing cancer risk In an enriched environment, new neurons are produced by the hippocampus, which then turns short-term memories to long-term ones. Moderate activity, for example walking and tai chi, also produces new neurons in the hippocampus and increases hippocampus volume, thus improving memory Walking forwards into landscapes thus creates long-term memories; walking has also been shown to protect against the neurodegeneration that causes Parkinson's Disease (PD) and Huntington's Disease, delaying the onset of dementias by ten years. A sedentary, immobile lifestyle is less stimulating, causing parts of the brain to atrophy. A central problem in PD is inactivity, and medical treatment encourages passivity. Walking can help to cure it but may take a high degree of concentration to bring habits from the bottom brain to the top Exercise in natural places is as effective as fluoxetine (e.g., Prozac) for many people and tranquil scenes can quieten the mind

For better health and well-being, many people thus need behaviours that increase both memory- and place-making. Places are dense with meaning, stories, memories, and morals. They work on your mind the contours of our minds are shaped by places. Both gardening and allomothering promote recovery from stress and improve well-being; members of allotment groups experience less stress than same-age members of indoor groups Location can improve health, especially if the place is culturally considered as home Aboriginal groups returning to outstations have seen reductions in hypertension and diabetes Changes in well-being have been noted for Innu groups returning to the land in Labrador Aboriginal people describe land as a spiritual place, calm and centred, where the "quietness speaks to you" Natural and physically sensate environments appear to give more opportunities for immersive attention where there is a mix of mild continuing stimulation of the SNS and majority control by the calming PNS. Simms and Potts have argued for a new materialism in which is cultured a more pleasurable and respectful relationship with the world of things. Experiential purchases produce more enduring happiness than material purchase, with consumers deriving more benefits from anticipation, from the doing-experience, and from the memories created Finding fault with material consumption may appear to be seeking a return to living in a cave: it should not. The greater challenge is to increase individual well-being, reduce anxiety and depression, take more responsibility for the planet's future, and create an abundance of less

8. Linking Greener Minds to Contemplative and Greener Economies

Green Mind Theory offers an opportunity to link individual well-being to life behaviours and thus to whole economies. The future of the planet's natural capital relies on new patterns of material consumption that shift behaviours to sustainable consumption (activities that build natural capital rather than deplete it), and/or non-material consumption (activities with a light footprint on resources, but which deliver well-being, such as listening to bird song, gardening, talking, walking, and volunteering)

Green minds can build empathy and trust. They strengthen mirror neurons that show empathy, and oxytocin increases bonding between individuals and suppresses the red alert nature of the amygdala Some traditions call this increasing the circle of us, acknowledging the secret history of our enemies: they too feel sorrow and suffering, and ten thousand things may have caused them to act. A green and prosocial mind puts an emphasis on giving, contributing, and volunteering. Volunteers have higher well-being than non-volunteers, greater life satisfaction across the life course, and live two years longer than non-volunteers Empathy would have been highly selected within group and bands during hominid evolution, and we search for it today. In hospital settings, patients are already on red alert: they are anxious and worried. In the U.S., those surgeons sued the most do not make more mistakes, they were just unable to establish trust and empathy with patients Nurses and doctors who spend more time with patients smile and treat them as individuals and are themselves happier; those patients also recover more rapidly and need less pain control. Porsche is a component of many contemplative traditions: acute attention to and immersion in the present moment Porsche moves in two directions: inwards into the mind, and outwards to the natural world and other people. More equal societies do better for all; inequality is bad for all Optimists live 19% longer than pessimists, suggesting that expectations about the future affect current well-being A popular assumption for the past half century has been that increased material consumption and rising GDP inevitably increases well-being. There have been many technological improvements to lives, yet timeless consumer culture invents new pleasures, often producing more suffering from second arrows: either we cannot access apparent pleasures, or when we do have them, they deliver less than expected, rapidly losing their lustre. One priority is to redefine prosperity, and by substituting activities that improve social cohesion, mental and physical well-being, and memory creation, the impact on natural capital and ecosystem services could be reduced whilst improving well-being

Green growth and the green economy have become important targets for national and international organisations, including the OECD, UNEP, the World Bank, the Rio+20 conference, and the Global Green Growth Initiative UNEP defines the green economy as "resulting in human well-being and social equity, while significantly reducing environmental risks and ecological scarcities". To date, many countries acknowledge the need for greener economies, but few have acted significantly. Notable exceptions include: China's launch of eco-civilisation policies, Korea's building an advanced carbon economy, Kenya's use of feed-in-tariffs dramatically to increase renewable sources of energy, and Denmark's production of more energy from wind than it consumes nationally.

Greener economies will not look much like the current economy. They will be disruptive but less than the impact of severe climate change. The notion of a greener and prosocial economy further implies a cultural understanding of how much is enough A key challenge is how a mode of consumption based on enough not more can be created, so resulting in mass behaviours of enounces Wood et al. have demonstrated the value of gratitude to well-being, and how it arises both from the receipt of aid/support from others and from an internal appreciation of the positive aspects of life. They conclude that people would be better off spending time amassing friendships and appreciating what they have rather than seeking higher incomes and amassing material possessions. In greener economies, different forms of contemplative consumption will be valued, such as of storytelling, engaging with nature, and skill-based crafts. They tend to be cooperative, enhancing social capital formation and reducing inequity. This will bring positive feedbacks, as prosocial behaviours cause others to be prosocial, thus building social capital They offer four options to consumers: resist consumerism by opting out (e.g., downshifting, voluntary simplicity), retain possessions for longer (before replacement), make different choices (ethical or green consumerism), and substitute non-material consumption activities (e.g., nature consumption) [5]. Part of the solution for greener economies is the adoption of activities that lead to green minds. The Caerphilly Cohort Study has, though, shown that there was no change in the adoption of healthy behaviours by men over 30 years (commencing 1979): those with four of five behaviours (non-smoking, acceptable body mass, high fruit and vegetable consumption, regular activity, and low-moderate alcohol intake) delayed onset of heart disease by 12 years alongside reduced cognitive impairment and a delayed onset of dementia But those starting with low adoption did not change over time, even though public knowledge of these risks has grown. Kvaavik et al. showed in a population of 5000 adults that the adoption of healthy behaviours extended life by a mean of 12 years.

9. Priorities for Implementing Healthy Habits

What does the Green Mind concept suggest for instruction and implementation? We have observed that the future of the planet relies on substitution of non-material consumption, making more of activities with a light footprint, and the co-delivery of well-being. But the history of implementation of healthy habits in affluent countries is not encouraging. There are five levels for possible action: International agreements: these are rare, slow to implement, and easy to free-ride or undermine. National policies: few successes for whole populations, so far, though anti-smoking and seat-belt legislation are successes. Institutional and sectoral policies and practice: the potential for government, employers, and charitable organisations to change practices to affect large numbers of people, such as in education, mental health, social care, or hospitals.

Community actions and ceremonies: already widespread and manifested in local groups and rituals but undervalued and not yet widely used to improve well-being.

Voluntary actions of individuals: hard to sustain, though the most pushed by governments.

Elements 1 and 2 are hard to achieve, and 5 is often too easy to demand: it will be institutions and communities that are likely to reach the largest number of people quickly. We propose an emphasis on nature, social, and craft engagements in neighbourhoods, schools, care homes, and health care facilities (Table 3). Environmental organisations and charities have a vital role to play promoting healthy engagement with nature as part of their missions. Employers also can act by focusing on work-life balance, and activities that contribute to well-being. Core intervention priorities should thus centre on hard-to-reach populations and cohorts, and those for whom current policies and treatment are struggling to find solutions. This includes those in certain age groups, such as children and the elderly, and those suffering from lifestyle-related conditions, such as obesity, type 2 diabetes, loneliness, and mental ill-health. These interventions are variously called Nature-Based Interventions (NBIs), Wise Psychological Interventions (WPIs), and Positive Psychological Interventions and offer opportunities for individual as well as collective restoration

Table 3. Nature, social, and craft engagements that build the green mind.

Table

The risk of death is reduced and longevity increased through social group membership and social support through interesting and healthy diets through cognitive engagement with craft and mindfulness/spiritual activities through physically-active lifestyles, such as in the Sardinian mountains Okinawa Harvard alumni and Caerphilly men Combinations of all can lead to exceptional longevity It thus appears that extreme longevity is promoted by the habitual consumption of healthy food, daily physical activity, an engagement with nature, strong social capital, and cognitive engagement. These also offer the prospect of living well and with contentment.

We propose twelve research questions to focus action on children, adults, healthy longevity, and redesign.

9.1. Children

Young children are becoming increasingly socially-disconnected, inactive, and eating badly: what green mind interventions would work best for 5–11-year olds?

How protective would such interventions be across the life course?

9.2. Adults

How can immersive-attention activities be promoted to produce health and well-being improvements across whole populations (including the dissipation of unhealthy habits)?

What are the best policies for local and national governments to implement that would aid such adoption and desorption?

What priority activities and behaviours should be promoted at stressful transition points in the life course (moving schools, transition to university, becoming a parent, marriage and divorce, deaths of friends and relatives, retirement, transition to social care)?

9.3. Longevity

What green mind interventions offer the greatest efficacy for health outcomes in elderly populations and social care settings?

How can interventions based on outdoor activity, social interactions, good food, and cognitive engagement be best implemented?

What can be learned from cultures where healthy living continues into the 8th–11th decades of the life course (such as in the longevity hotspots of Nagano and Okinawa in Japan)?

9.4. Redesign

What well-being and health outcomes could be delivered in hospitals and care settings if green and prosocial design was implemented?

How much real income could be saved by hospitals from promoting behaviours that prevented the need for treatment?

How can human settlements be redesigned to increase engagement with existing green spaces?

Could some solutions to climate change rest in the green mind and its capacity to drive low consumption behaviours?

We conclude by setting out a ten-point call to action based on compelling supportive scientific evidence about the influence of lifestyle and behaviour on short- and long-term well-being (Table 4). None of this will be easy to achieve at the population level. It will require behaviour change and habit formation; it will require changes in infrastructure, policies, and resourcing. But every small contemplative undertaking can lead to the gradual formation of a green mind. It just needs relentless persistence long enough to form the habit. As indicated above, it will be institutions and communities that are likely to reach the largest number of people quickly. There could be emphasis on nature, social, and craft engagements in neighbourhoods, schools, care homes, and health care facilities. Environmental organisations and charities could play a vital role in promoting healthy engagement with nature as part of their missions. Every child could be outdoors every day; every older person in a care home could sit in a garden. Every economy could be green and prosocial. Now is time for a new ethic: the economy is the environment. Nature will survive us all.

Table 4. Ten calls to action for the green mind.

Table

Conclusions

Comments on the Green Mind

Nudge tactics and policy changes have now made it possible in some countries to imagine the reality of an entirely tobacco-free culture, or where some water and air systems are pollution-free. In others, hunger has been dramatically reduced. What level, thus, of ambition is possible when considering policies and practices that could mostly solve lifestyle-related conditions and diseases typical of modern, high material-consumption cultures, utilizing the Green Mind Theory? Is it possible to imagine substantial reductions in incidence of mental ill-health, obesity, type 2 diabetes, loneliness, physical inactivity, and cardiovascular disease through the adoption of resilient green mind habits, fostering prosocial and greener economies across whole populations? We suggest Green Mind Theory offers some new opportunities to address these pervasive challenges by suggesting new routes to raising the well-being baseline of whole populations though the adoption of healthier habits and behaviours.

Theory of Mind

Theory of Mind is the branch of cognitive science that investigates how we ascribe mental states to other persons and how we use the states to explain and predict the actions of those other persons. More accurately, it is the branch that investigates mindreading or mentalizing or mentalistic abilities. These skills are shared by almost all human beings beyond early childhood. They are used to treat other agents as the bearers of unobservable psychological states and processes, and to anticipate and explain the agents' behaviour in terms of such states and processes. These mentalistic abilities are also called "folk psychology" by philosophers, and "naïve psychology" and "intuitive psychology" by cognitive scientists. It is important to note that Theory of Mind is not an appropriate term to characterize this research area (and neither to denote our mentalistic abilities) since it seems to assume right from the start the validity of a specific account of the nature and development of mindreading, that is, the view that it depends on the deployment of a theory of the mental realm, analogous to the theories of the physical world ("naïve physics"). But this view—known as theory-theory—is only one of the accounts offered to explain our mentalistic abilities. In contrast, theorists of mental simulation have suggested that what lies at the root of mindreading is not any sort of folk-psychological conceptual scheme, but rather a kind of mental modelling in which the simulator uses her own mind as an analogy model of the mind of the simulated agent. Both theory-theory and simulation-theory are families of theories. Some theory-theorists maintain that our naïve theory of mind is the product of the scientific-like exercise of a domain-general theorizing capacity. Other theory-theorists defend a quite different hypothesis, according to which mindreading rests on the maturation of a mental organ dedicated to the domain of psychology. Simulation-theory also shows different facets. According to the "moderate" version of simulations, mental concepts are not completely excluded from simulation. Simulation be a process through which we first generate, and self-attribute pretend mental states that are intended to correspond to those of the simulated agent, and then project them onto the target. By contrast, the "radical" version of simulations rejects the primacy of first-person mindreading and contends that we imaginatively transform ourselves into the simulated agent, interpreting the target's behaviour without using any kind of mental concept, not even ones referring to ourselves. Finally, the claim common to both theorists of theory and theorists of simulation that mindreading plays a primary role in human social understanding was challenged in the early 21st century, mainly by phenomenology-oriented philosophers and cognitive scientists.

Table of Contents

Theory-

The Child-Scientist Theory

The Modularise Theory-

First-Person Mindreading and Theory-

Simulation-Theory

Simulation with and without Introspection

Simulation in Low-Level Mindreading

Social Cognition without Mindreading

References and Further Reading

Suggested Further Reading

References

1. Theory-

Social psychologists have investigated mindreading since at least the 1940s. In Heider and Simmel's (1944) classic studies, participants were presented with animated events involving interacting geometric shapes. When asked to report what they saw, the participants almost invariably treated these shapes as intentional agents with motives and purposes, suggesting the existence of an automatic capacity for mentalistic attribution. Pursuing this line of research would lead to Heider's The Psychology of Interpersonal Relations (1958), a seminal book which is one of the main historical referents of the scientific inquiry into our mentalistic practice. In this book Heider characterizes "common sense psychology" as a sophisticated conceptual scheme that has an influence on human perception and action in the social world comparable to that which Kant's categorical framework has on human perception and action in the physical world (see Male & Ickes 2000: 201).

Heider's visionary work played a central role in the origination and definition of attribution theory, that is, the field of social psychology that investigates the mechanisms underlying ordinary explanations of our own and other people's behaviour. However, attribution theory is a quite different way of approaching our mentalistic practice. Heider took common sense psychology in its real value of knowledge, arguing that scientific psychology has a good deal to learn from it. In contrast, most research on causal attribution has been faithful to behaviourism's methodological lesson and focused on the epistemic inaccuracy of common-sense psychology. Two years before Heider's book, Wilfred Sellars' (1956) Empiricism and the Philosophy of Mind had suggested that our grasp of mental phenomena does not originate from direct access to our inner life, but is the result of a "folk" theory of mind, which we acquire through some form or other of enculturation. Sellars' speculation turned out to be very philosophically productive and in agreement with social-psychology research on self-attribution, coming to be known as "Theory-Theory" (a term coined by Morton 1980—henceforth "TT"). During the 1970s one or other form of TT was a very effective antidote to Cartesians and philosophical behaviourism. In particular, TT was coupled with Nagel's (1961) classic account of intertheoretical reduction as deduction of the reduced from the reducing theory via bridge principles in order to turn the ontological problem of the relationship between the mental and the physical into a more tractable epistemological problem concerning the relations between theories. Thus it became possible to take a notion—intertheoretical reduction—rigorously studied by philosophers of science; to examine the relations between folk psychology as a theory including the common sense mentalistic ontology and its scientific successors (scientific psychology, neuroscience, or some other form of science of the mental); and to let ontological/metaphysical questions be answered by (I) focusing on questions about explanation and theory reduction first and foremost, and then (ii) depending on how those first questions were answered, drawing the appropriate ontological/metaphysical conclusions based on a comparison with how similar questions about explanation and reduction got answered in other scientific episodes and the ontological conclusions philosophers and scientists drew in those cases (this strategy is labelled "the intertheoretical-reduction reformulation of the mind-body problem" in Buckle 2003). In this context, TT was taken as the major premise in the standard argument for eliminative materialism (see Ramsey 2011: §2.1). In its strongest form, eliminative predicts that part or all of our folk-psychological theory will vanish into thin air, just as it happened in the past when scientific progress led to the abandonment of the folk theory of witchcraft or the prescientific theories of phlogiston and caloric fluid. This prediction rests on an argument which moves from considering folk psychology as a massively defective theory to the conclusion that—just as with witches, phlogiston, and caloric fluid—folk-psychological entities do not exist. Thus philosophy of mind joined attribution theory in adopting a critical attitude toward the explanatory adequacy of folk psychology (see, for example, Stich's 1983 eliminability doubts about the folk concept of belief, motivated inter alia by the experimental social psychology literature on dissonance and self-attribution). Notice, however, that TT can be differently construed depending on whether we adopt a personal or sub personal perspective (see Stich & Ravenscroft 1994: §4). The debate between intentional realists and eliminative favoured David Lewis' personal-level formulation of TT. According to Lewis, the folk theory of mind is implicit in our everyday talk about mental states. We entertain "platitudes" regarding the causal relations of mental states, sensory stimuli, and motor responses that can be systematized (or "Ramified"). The result is a functionalist theory that gives the terms of mentalistic vocabulary their meaning in the same way as scientific theories define their theoretical terms, namely "as the occupants of the causal roles specified by the theory…; as the entities, whatever those may be, that bear certain causal relations to one another and to the referents of the O[observational]-terms" (Lewis 1972: 211). In this perspective, mindreading can be described as an exercise in reflective reasoning, which involves the application of general reasoning abilities to premises including ceteris paribus folk-psychological generalizations. A good example of this conception of mindreading is Grice's schema for the derivation of conversational implicatures: He said that P; he could not have done this unless he thought that Q; he knows (and knows that I know that he knows) that I will realize that it is necessary to suppose that Q; he has done nothing to stop me thinking that Q; so he intends me to think, or is at least willing for me to think, that Q(Grice 1989: 30-1; cit. in Wilson 2005: 1133). Since the end of the 1970s, however, primatology, developmental psychology, cognitive neuropsychiatry, and empirically informed philosophy have been contributing to a collaborative inquiry into TT. In the context of this literature the term "theory" refers to a "tacit" or "sub-doxastic" structure of knowledge, a corpus of internally represented information that guides the execution of mentalistic capacities. But then the functionalist theory that fixes the meaning of mentalistic terms is not the theory implicit in our everyday, mentalistic talk, but the tacit theory (in Chomsky's sense) sub serving our thought and talk about the mental realm (see Stich & Nichols 2003: 241). On this perspective, the inferential processes that depend on the theory have an automatic and unconscious character that distinguishes them from reflective reasoning processes. In developmental psychology part of the basis for the study of mindreading skills in children was already in Jean Piaget's seminal work on egocentrism in the 1930s to 50s, and the work on metacognition (especially metamemory) in the 1970s. But the developmental research on mindreading took off only under the thrust of three discoveries in the 1980s (see Leslie 1998). First, normally developing 2-year-olds can engage in pretend play. Second, normally developing children undergo a deep change in their understanding of the psychological states of other people somewhere between the ages of 3 and 4, as indicated especially by the appearance of their ability to solve a variety of "false-belief" problems (see immediately below). Lastly, children diagnosed with autism spectrum disorders are especially impaired in attributing mental states to other people. Swimmer & Penner (1983) provided the theory-of-mind research with a seminal experimental paradigm: the "false-belief task." In the most well-known version of this task, a child watches two puppets interacting in a room. One puppet ("Sally") puts a toy in location A and then leaves the room. While Sally is out of the room, the other puppet ("Anne") moves the toy from location A to location B. Sally returns to the room, and the child onlooker is asked where she will look for her toy, in location A or in location B. Now, 4- and 5-year-olds have little difficulty passing this test, judging that Sally will look for her toy in location A although it really is in location B. These correct answers provide evidence that the child realizes that Sally does not know that the toy has been moved, and so will act upon a false belief. Many younger children, typically 3-year-olds, fail such a task, often asserting that Sally will look for the toy in the place where it was moved. Dozens of versions of this task have now been used, and while the precise age of success varies between children and between task versions, in general we can confidently say that children begin to successfully perform the ("verbal") false-belief tasks at around 4 years (see the meta-analysis in Wellman et al. 2001; see also below, the reference to "non-verbal" false-belief tasks).

Swimmer and Penner's false-belief task set off a flood of experiments concerning the infant understanding of the mind. In this context, the first hypotheses about the process of acquisition of the naïve theory of mind were suggested. The finding that mentalistic skills emerge very early, in the first 3-4 years, and in a way relatively independent from the development of other cognitive abilities, led some scholars (for example, Simon Baron-Cohen, Jerry Feodor, Alan Leslie) to conceive them as the end-state of the endogenous maturation of an innate theory-of-mind module (or system of modules). This contrasted with the view of other researchers (for example, Alison Gopnik, Josef Penner, Henry Wellman), who maintained that the intuitive theory of mind develops in childhood in a manner comparable to the development of scientific theories.

a. The Child-Scientist Theory

According to a first version of TT, "the child (as little) scientist theory," the body of internally-represented knowledge that drives the exercise of mentalistic abilities has much the same structure as a scientific theory, and it is acquired, stored, and used in much the same way that scientific theories are: by formulating explanations, making predictions, and then revising the theory or modifying auxiliary hypotheses when the predictions fail. Gopnik & Meltzoff (1997) put forward this idea in its more radical form. They argue that the body of knowledge underlying mindreading has all the structural, functional, and dynamic features that, on their view, characterize most scientific theories. One of the most important features is defeasibility. As it happens in scientific practice, the child's naïve theory of mind can also be "annulled," that is, replaced when an accumulation of counterevidence to it occurs. The child-scientist theory is, therefore, akin to Piaget's constructivism insofar as it depicts the cognitive development in childhood and early adolescence as a succession of increasingly sophisticated naïve theories. For instance, Wellman (1990) has argued that around age 4 children become able to pass the false-belief tests because they move from an elementary "copy" theory of mind to a fully "representational" theory of mind, which allows them to acknowledge the explanatory role of false beliefs. The child-scientist theory inherits from Piaget not only the constructivist framework but also the idea that the cognitive development is a process that depends on a domain-general learning mechanism. A domain-general (or general-purpose) psychological structure is one that can be used to do problem solving across many different content domains; it contrasts with a domain-specific psychological structure, which is dedicated to solving a restricted class of problems in a restricted content domain (see Samuels 2000). Now, Piaget's model of cognitive development posits an innate endowment of reflexes and domain-general learning mechanisms, which enable the child to set up sensorimotor interactions with the environment that unfold a steady improvement in the capacity of problem-solving in any cognitive domain—physical, biological, psychological, and so forth. Analogously, Gopnik & Schulz (2004, 2007) have argued that the learning mechanism that supports all cognitive development is a domain-general Bayesian mechanism that allows children to extract causal structure from patterns of data. Another theory-theorist who endorses a domain-general conception of cognitive development is Josef Penner (1991). On his view, it is the appearance of the ability to meet represent that enables the 4-year-olds to shift from a "situation theory" to a "representation theory," and thus pass false-belief tests. Children are situation theorists by the age of around 2 years. At 3 they possess a concept, "prolife" (or "bedance"), in which the concepts of pretend and belief coexist undifferentiated. The concept of prolife allows the child to understand that a person can "act as if" something was such and such (for example, as if "this banana is a telephone") when it is not. At 4 children acquire a representational concept of belief which enables them to understand that, like the public representations, inner representations can also misrepresent states of affairs (see Penner, Baker & Hutton 1994). Thus, Penner suggests that children first learn to understand the properties of public (pictorial and linguistic) representations; only in a second moment they extend, through a process of analogical reasoning, these characteristics to mental representations. On this perspective, then, the concept of belief is the product of a domain-general metarepresentational capacity that includes but is not limited to metarepresentational of mental states. (But for criticism, see Harris 2000, who argues that pretence and belief are very different and are readily distinguished by context by 3-year olds.)

b. The Modularise Theory-

According to the child-scientist theory, children learn the naïve theory of mind in much the same way that adults learn about scientific theories. By contrast, the modularise version of TT holds that the body of knowledge underlying mindreading lacks the structure of a scientific theory, being stored in one or more innate modules, which gradually become functional ("mature") during infant development. Inside the module the body of information can be stored as a suite of domain-specific computational mechanisms; or as a system of domain-specific representations; or in both ways (see Simpson et al. 2005: 13).

The notion of modularity as domain-specificity, whose paradigm is Noam Chomsky's module of language, informs the so-called "core knowledge" hypothesis, according to which human cognition builds on a repertoire of domain-specific systems of knowledge. Studies of children and adults in diverse cultures, human infants, and non-human primates provide evidence for at least four systems of knowledge that serve to represent significant aspects of the environment: inanimate objects and their motions; agents and their goal-directed actions; places and their geometric relations; sets and their approximate numerical relation. These are systems of domain-specific, task-specific representations, which are shared by other animals, persist in adults, and show little variation by culture, language, or sex (see Carey & Selke 1996; Selke & Kindler 2007).

And yet a domain-specific body of knowledge is an "inert" psychological structure, which gives rise to behaviour only if it is manipulated by some cognitive mechanism. The question arises, then, whether the domain-specific body of information that sub serves mentalistic abilities is the database of either a domain-specific or domain-general computational system. In some domains, a domain-specific computational mechanism and a domain-specific body of information can form a single mechanism (for example, a parser is very likely to be a domain-specific computational mechanism that manipulates a domain-specific data structure). But in other domains, as Samuels (1998, 2000) has noticed, domain-specific systems of knowledge might be computed by domain-general rather than domain-specific algorithms (but for criticism, see Carruthers 2006 The existence of a domain-specific algorithm that exploits a body of information specific to the domain of naïve psychology has been proposed by Alan Leslie (1994, 2000). He postulated a specialized component of social intelligence, the "Theory-of-Mind Mechanism" (Tommy), which receives as input information about the past and present behaviour of other people and utilizes this information to compute their probable psychological states. The outputs of Tommy are descriptions of psychological states in the form of met representations or M-representations, that is, agent-cantered descriptions of behaviour, which include a triadic relation that specifies four kinds of information: (I) an agent, (ii) an informational relation that specifies the agent's attitude (pretending, believing, desiring, and so forth), (iii) an aspect of reality that grounds the agent's attitude, (iv) the content of the agent's attitude. Therefore, to pretend and understand others' pretending, the child's Tommy is supposed to output the M-representation <Mother PRETENDS (of) this banana (that) "it is a telephone">. Analogously, to predict Sally's behaviour in the false-belief test, Tommy is supposed to output the M-representation <Sally BELIEVES (of) her marble (that) "it is in the basket">. (Note that Leslie coined the term "M-representation" to distinguish his own concept of meta-representation from Penner's 1991. For Penner uses the term at a personal level to refer to the child's conscious theory of representation, whereas Leslie utilizes the term at a sub personal level to designate an unconscious data structure computed by an information-processing mechanism. See Leslie & Thais 1992: 231, note 2.) In the 1980s, Leslie's Tommy hypothesis was the basis for the development of a neuropsychological perspective on autism. Children suffering from this neurodevelopmental disorder exhibit a triad of impairments: social incompetence, poor verbal and nonverbal communicative skills, and a lack of pretend play. Because social competence, communication, and pretending all rest on mentalistic abilities, Baron-Cohen, Frith & Leslie (1985) speculated that the autistic triad might be the result of an impaired Tommy. This hypothesis was investigated in an experiment in which typically developing 4-year-olds, children with autism (12 years; IQ 82), and children with Down syndrome (10 years; IQ 64) were tested on the Sally and Ann false-belief task. Eighty-five percent of the normally developing children and 86% of the children with Down syndrome passed the test; but only 20% of the autistic children predicted that Sally would look in the basket. This is one of the first examples of psychiatry driven by cognitive neuropsychology (followed by Christopher Frith's 1992 theory of schizophrenia as late-onset autism). According to Leslie, the Tommy is the specific innate basis of basic mentalistic abilities, which matures during the infant's second year. In support of this hypothesis, he cites inter alia his analysis of pretend play that would show that 18-month-old children are able to meet represent the propositional attitude of pretending. This analysis results, however, in an immediate empirical problem. If the Tommy is fully functional at 18 months, why are children unable to successfully perform false-belief tasks until they are around 4 years old? Leslie's hypothesis is that although the concept of belief is already in place in children younger than 4, in the false-belief tasks this concept is masked by immaturity in another capacity that is necessary for good performance on the task—namely inhibitory control. Since, by default, the Tommy attributes a belief with content that reflects current reality, to succeed in a false-belief task this default attribution must be inhibited and an alternative nonfactual content for the belief selected instead. This is the task of an executive control mechanism that Leslie calls "Selection Processor" (SP). Thus 3-year-olds fail standard false-belief tasks because they possess the Tommy but not yet the inhibitory SP (see Leslie & Thais 1992; Leslie & Palazzi 1998). The Tommy/SP model seems to find support in a series of experiments that test understanding of false mental and public representations in normal and autistic children. Leslie & Thais (1992) have found that normal 3-year-olds fail the standard false-belief tasks, the two non-mental meta-representational tests, the false-map task and Zaitchik's (1990) outdated-photograph task. In contrast, autistic children are at or near ceiling on the non-mental metarepresentational tests but fail false-belief tasks. Normal 4-year-olds can succeed in all these tasks. According to Leslie and Thais, the Tommy/SP model can account for these findings: normal 3-year-olds possess the Tommy but not yet SP; autistic children are impaired in Tommy but not in SP; normal 4-year-olds possess both the Tommy and an adequate SP. By contrast, these results appear to be counterevidence to Penner's idea that children first understand public representations before then applying that understanding to mental states. If this were right, then autistic children should have difficulty with both kinds of representations. And in fact Penner (1993) suggests that the autistic deficit is due to a genetic impairment of the mechanisms that sub serve attention shifting, a damage that interferes with the formation of the database required for the development of a theory of representation in general. But what autistics' performance in mental and non-mental metarepresentational tasks seems to show is a dissociation between understanding false maps and outdated photographs, on one hand, and understanding false beliefs, on the other. A finding that can be easily explained in the context of Leslie's domain-specific approach to mindreading, according to which children with autism have a specific deficit in understanding mental representation but not representation in general. In support of this interpretation, fMRI studies showed that activity in the right temporo-parietal junction is high while participants are thinking about false beliefs, but no different from resting levels while participants are thinking about outdated photographs or false maps or signs. This suggests a neural substrate for the behavioural dissociation between pictorial and mental metarepresentational abilities (see Saxe & Kanwisher 2003; for a critical discussion of the domain-specificity interpretation of these behavioural and neuroimaging data, see Germans & Stone 2008; Penner & Eichhorn 2008; Penner & Leek am 2008). Leslie (2005) recruits new data to support his claim that mental metarepresentational abilities emerge from a specialized neurocognitive mechanism that matures during the second year of life. Standard false-belief tasks are "elicited-response" tasks in which children are asked a direct question about an agent's false belief. But investigations using "spontaneous-response" tasks (Oishi & Baillargeon 2005) seem to suggest that the ability to attribute false beliefs is present much earlier, at the age of 15 months (even at 13 months in Saurian, Cali & Sperber 2007). However, Leslie's mentalistic interpretation of these data has been challenged by Ruffman & Penner (2005), who have proposed an explanation of Oishi and Baillargeon's results that assumes that the infants might be employing a non-mentalistic behaviour-rule such as, "People look for objects where last seen" (for replies, see Baillargeon et al. 2010). The Tommy has been considered, contra Feodor, as one of the strongest candidates for central modularity (see, for example, Cotterill & Carruthers 1999: 67-8). However, Samuels (2006: 47) has objected that it is difficult to establish whether the Tommy's domain of application is central cognition. He suggests that the question is still more controversial in light of Leslie's proposal of modelling Tommy as a relatively low-level mechanism of selective attention, whose functioning depends on SP, which is a non-modular mechanism, penetrable to knowledge and instruction (see Leslie, Friedman & German 2004).

c. First-Person Mindreading and Theory-During the 1980s and 1990s most of the work in Theory of Mind was concerned with the mechanisms that sub serve the attribution of psychological states to others (third-person mindreading). In the last decade, however, an increasing number of psychologists and philosophers have also proposed accounts of the mechanisms underlying the attribution of psychological states to oneself (first-person mindreading). For most theory-theorists, first-person mindreading is an interpretative activity that depends on mechanisms that capitalize on the same theory of mind used to attribute mental states to other agents. Such mechanisms are triggered by information about mind-external states of affairs, essentially the target's behaviour and/or the situation in which it occurs/occurred. The claim is, then, that there is a functional symmetry between first-person and third-person mentalistic attribution—the "outside access" view of introspection in Robbins the "symmetrical" or "self/other parity" account of self-knowledge in Schnitzel (2010).

The first example of a symmetrical account of self-knowledge is Beam's (1972) "self-perception theory." With reference to Skinner's methodological guidance, but with a position that reveals affinities with symbolic interactionism, Bam holds that one knows one's own inner states (for example, attitudes and emotions) through a process completely analogous to that occurring when one knows other people' inner states, that is, by inferring them from the observation/recollection of one's own behaviour and/or the circumstances in which it occurs/occurred. The

TT version of the symmetrical account of self-knowledge develops Beam's approach by claiming that observations and recollections of one's own behaviour and the circumstances in which it occurs/occurred are the input of mechanisms that exploit theories that apply to the same extent to ourselves and to others. In the well-known social-psychology experiments reviewed by Nisbett & Wilson (1977), the participants' attitudes and behaviour were caused by motivational factors inaccessible to consciousness—such factors as cognitive dissonance, numbers of bystanders in a public crisis, positional and "halo" effects and subliminal cues in problem solving and semantic disambiguation, and so on. However, when explicitly asked about the motivations (causes) of their actions, the subjects did not hesitate to state, sometimes with great eloquence, their very reasonable motives. Nisbett and Wilson explained this pattern of results by arguing that the subjects did not have any direct access to the real causes of their attitudes and behaviour; rather, they engaged in an activity of confabulation, that is, they exploited a priori causal theories to develop reasonable but imaginary explanations of the motivational factors of their attitudes and behaviour (see also Johansson et al. 2006, where Nisbett and Wilson's legacy is developed through a new experimental paradigm to study introspection, the "choice blindness" paradigm). Evidence for the symmetrical account of self-knowledge comes from Nisbett & Bellows' (1977) utilization of the so-called "actor-observer paradigm." In one experiment they compared the introspective reports of participants ("actors") to the reports of a control group of "observers" who were given a general description of the situation and asked to predict how the actors would react. Observers' predictions were found to be statistically identical to—and as inaccurate as—the reports by the actors. This finding suggests that "both groups produced these reports via the same route, namely by applying or generating similar causal theories" (Nisbett & Wilson 1977: 250-1; see also Schnitzel 2010: §§2.1.2 and 4.2.1).

In developmental psychology Alison Gopnik (1993) has defended a symmetrical account of self-knowledge by arguing that there is good developmental evidence of developmental synchronies: children's understanding of themselves proceeds in lockstep with their understanding of others. For example, since TT assumes that first-person and third-person mentalistic attributions are both sub served by the same theory of mind, it predicts that if the theory is not yet equipped to solve certain third-person false-belief problems, then the child should also be unable to perform the parallel first-person task. A much-discussed instance of parallel performance on tasks for self and other is in Gopnik & Astington (1988). In the "Smarties Box" experiment, children were shown with the candy container for the British confection "Smarties" and were asked what they thought was in the container. Naturally they answered "Smarties." The container was then opened to reveal not Smarties, but a pencil.

Children were then asked a series of questions, including "What will [your friend] say is in the box?", and successively "When you first saw the box, before we opened it, what did you think was inside it?". It turned out that the children's ability to answer the question concerning oneself was significantly correlated with their ability to answer the question concerning another. (See also the above-cited Wellman et al. 2001, which offers meta-analytic findings to the effect that performance on false-belief tasks for self and for others is virtually identical at all ages.) Data from autism have also been used to motivate the claim that first-person and third person mentalistic attribution has a common basis. An intensely debated piece of evidence comes from a study by Hurlburt, Happen & Frith (1994), in which three people suffering from Asperger syndrome were tested with the descriptive experience sampling method. In this experimental paradigm, subjects are instructed to carry a random beeper, pay attention to the experience that was ongoing at the moment of the beep, and jot down notes about that now-immediately-past experience (see Hurlburt & Schnitzel 2007). The study showed marked qualitative differences in introspection in the autistic subjects: unlike normal subjects who report several different phenomenal state types—including inner verbalisation, visual images, unsymbolised thinking, and emotional feelings—the first two autistic subjects reported visual images only; the third subject could report no inner experience at all. According to Frith & Happen (1999: 14), this evidence strengthens the hypothesis that self-awareness, like other awareness, is dependent on the same theory of mind. Thus, evidence from social psychology, development psychology and cognitive neuropsychiatry makes a case for a symmetrical account of self-knowledge. As Schnitzel (2010: §2.1.3) rightly notes, however, no one advocates a thoroughly symmetrical conception because some margin is always left for some sort of direct self-knowledge. Nisbett & Wilson (1977: 255), for example, draw a sharp distinction between "cognitive processes" (the causal processes underlying judgments, decisions, emotions, sensations) and mental "content" (those judgments, decisions, emotions, sensations themselves). Subjects have "direct access" to this mental content, and this allows them to know it "with near certainty." In contrast, they have no access to the processes that cause behaviour. However, insofar as Nisbett and Wilson do not propose any hypothesis about this alleged direct self-knowledge, their theory is incomplete.

In order to offer an account of this supposedly direct self-knowledge, some philosophers made a more or less radical return to various forms of Cartesians, construing first-person mindreading as a process that permits the access to at least some mental phenomena in a relatively direct and non-interpretative way. On this perspective, introspective access does not appeal to theories that serve to interpret "external" information, but rather exploits mechanisms that can receive information about inner life through a relatively direct channel—

the "inside access" view of introspection in Robbins (2006: 618); the "self-detection" account of self-knowledge in Schnitzel (2010: §2.2). The inside access view comes in various forms. Mentalistic self-attribution may be realized by a mechanism that processes information about the functional profile of mental states, or their representational content, or both kinds of information (see Robbins 2006: 618; for a "neural" version of the inside access view, see below, §2a). A representationalism-functionalist version of the inside access view is Nichols & Stich's (2003) account of first-person mindreading in terms of "monitoring mechanisms." The authors begin by drawing a distinction between detection and inference. It is one thing to detect mental states, it is another to reason about mental states, that is, using information about mental states to predict and explain one's own or other people's mental states and behaviour. Moreover, both the attribution of a mental state and the inferences that one can make about it can be referred to oneself or other people. Thus, we get four possible operations: first- and third-person detection, first- and third-person reasoning. Now, Nichols and Stich's hypothesis is that whereas third-person detecting and first- and third-person reasoning are all sub served by the same theory of mind, the mechanism for detecting one's own mental states is quite independent of the mechanism that deals with the mental states of other people. More precisely, the Monitoring Mechanism (MM) theory assumes the existence of a suite of distinct self-monitoring computational mechanisms, including one for monitoring and providing self-knowledge of one's own experiential states, and one for monitoring and providing self-knowledge of one's own propositional attitudes. Thus, for example, if X believes that p, and the proper MM is activated, it copies the representation p in X's "Belief Box", embeds the copy in a representation schema of the form "I believe that and then places this second-order representation back in X's Belief Box. Since the MM theory assumes that first-person mindreading does not involve mechanisms of the sort that figure in third-person mindreading, it implies that the first capacity should be dissociable, both diachronically and synchronically, from the second. In support of this prediction Nichols & Stich (2003) cite developmental data to the effect that, on a wide range of tasks, instead of the parallel performance predicted by TT, children exhibit developmental asynchronies. For example, children are capable of attributing knowledge and ignorance to themselves before they can attribute those states to others (Swimmer et al. 1988). Moreover, they suggest—on the basis, inter alia, of a reinterpretation of the aforementioned Hurlburt, Happen & Frith's (1994) data—that there is some evidence of a double dissociation between schizophrenic and autistic subjects: the MMs might be intact in autistics despite their impairment in third-person mindreading; in schizophrenics the pattern might be reversed. The MM theory provides a neo-Cartesian reply to TT—and especially to its eliminative implications since the mentalistic self-attributions based on MMs are immune to the potentially distorting influence of our intuitive theory of psychology. However, the MM theory faces at least two difficulties. To start with, the theory must tell us how MM establishes which attitude type (or percept type) a given mental state belongs to (Goldman 2006: 238-9). A possibility is that there is a separate MM for each propositional attitude type and for each perceptual modality. But then, as Engelbart and Carruthers (2010: 246) remark, since any MM can be selectively impaired, the MM theory predicts a multitude of dissociations—for example, subjects who can self-attribute beliefs but not desires, or visual experiences but not auditory ones, and so on. However, the hypothesis of such a massive disposability has little empirical plausibility.

Moreover, Carruthers (2011) has offered a book-length argument against the idea of a direct access to propositional attitudes. His neurocognitive framework is Bernard Bars' Global Workspace Theory model of consciousness (see Gennaro 2005: §4c), in which a range of perceptual systems "broadcast" their outputs (for example, sensory data from the environment, imagery, somatosensory and proprioceptive data) to a complex of conceptual systems (judgment-forming, memory-forming, desire-forming, decision-making systems, and so forth). Among the conceptual systems there is also a multi-componential "mindreading system," which generates higher-order judgments about the mental states of others and of oneself. By virtue of receiving globally broadcast perceptual states as input, the mindreading system can easily recognize those precepts, generating self-attributions of the form "I see something red," "It hurts," and so on. But the system receives no input from the systems that generate propositional attitude events (like judging and deciding). Consequently, the mindreading system cannot directly self-attribute propositional attitude events; it must infer them by exploiting the perceptual input (together with the outputs of various memory systems). Thus, Carruthers (2009: 124) concludes, "self-attributions of propositional attitude events like judging and deciding are always the result of a swift (and unconscious) process of self-interpretation." On this perspective, therefore, we do not introspect our own propositional attitude events. Our only form of access to those events is via self-interpretation, turning our mindreading faculty upon ourselves and engaging in unconscious interpretation of our own behaviour, physical circumstances, and sensory events like visual imagery and inner speech. Carruthers bases his proposal on considerations to do with the evolution of mindreading and metacognition, the rejection of the above-cited data that according to Nichols & Stich (2003) suggest developmental asynchronies and dissociation between self-attribution and other-attribution, and on evidence about the confabulation of attitudes. Thus, Carruthers develops a very sophisticated version of the symmetrical account of self-knowledge in which the theory-driven mechanisms underlying first- and third-person mindreading can count not only on observations and recollections of one's own behaviour and the circumstances in which it occurs/occurred, but also on the recognition of a multitude of perceptual and quasi-perceptual events.

2. Simulation-Theory

Until the mid-1980s the debate on the nature of mindreading was a debate between the different variants of TT. But in 1986, TT was impugned by Robert Gordon and, independently, by Jane Heal, who gave life to an alternative which was termed "simulation-theory" (ST). In 1989 Alvin Goldman and Paul Harris began to contribute to this new approach to mindreading. In 2006, Goldman provided the most thoroughly developed, empirically supported defines of a simulations account of our mentalistic abilities. According to ST, our third-person mindreading ability does not consist in implicit theorizing but rather in representing the psychological states and processes of others by mentally simulating them, that is, attempting to generate similar states and processes in ourselves. Thus, the same resources that are used in our own psychological states and processes are recycled—usually but not only in imagination—to provide an understanding of psychological states and processes of the simulated target. This has often been compared to the method of Einfühlung exalted by the theorists of Verstehen (see Stieber 2006: 5-19). For a mind reader to engage in this process of imaginative recycling, various information processing mechanisms are needed. The mind reader simulates the psychological ethology of the actions of the target in essentially two steps. First, the simulator generates pretend or imaginary mental states in her own mind which are intended to (at least partly) correspond to those of the target. Second, the simulator feeds the imaginary states into a suitable cognitive mechanism (for example, the decision-making system) that is taken "offline," that is, it is disengaged from the motor control systems. If the simulator's decision-making system is similar to the target's one, and the pretend mental states that the simulator introduces into the decision-making system (at least partly) match the target's, then the output of the simulator's decision-making system might reliably be attributed or assigned to the target. On this perspective, there is no need for an internally represented knowledge base and there is no need of a naïve theory of psychology. The simulator exploits a part of her cognitive apparatus as a model for a part of the simulated agent's cognitive apparatus. Hence follows one of the main advantages ST is supposed to have over TT—namely its computational parsimony. According to advocates of ST, the body of tacit folk-psychological knowledge which TT attributes to mind readers imposes too heavy a burden on mental computation. However, such a load will diminish radically if, instead of computing the body of knowledge posited by TT, mind readers must only co-opt mechanisms that are primarily used online, when they experience a kind of mental state, to run offline simulations of similar states in the target (the argument is suggested by Gordon 1986 and Goldman 1995, and challenged by Stich & Nichols 1992, 1995).

In the early years of the debate over ST, a focus was on its implications for the controversy between intentional realism and eliminative materialism. Gordon (1986) and Goldman (1989) suggested that by rejecting the assumption that folk psychology is a theory, ST undercuts eliminative. Stich & Ravenscroft (1994: §5), however, objected that ST undermines eliminative only provided that the latter adopts the sub personal version of TT. For ST does not deny the evident fact that human beings have intuitions about the mental, and neither rules out that such intuitions might be systematized by building, as David Lewis suggests, a theory that implies them. Consequently, ST does not refute eliminative; it instead forces the eliminative to include among the premises of her argument Lewis' personal formulation of TT, together with the observation/prediction that the theory implicit in our everyday talk about mental states is or will turn out to be seriously defective. One of the main objections that theory-theorists raise against ST is the argument from systematic errors in prediction. According to ST errors in prediction can arise either (I) because the predictor's executive system is different from that of the target, or (ii) because the pretend mental states that the predictor has introduced into the executive system do not match the ones that actually motivate the target. However, Stich & Nichols (1992, 1995; see also Nichols et al. 1996) describe experimental situations in which the participants systematically fail to predict the behaviour of targets, and in which it is unlikely that (I) or (ii) is the source of problem. Now, TT can easily explain such systematic errors in prediction: it is sufficient to assume that our naïve theory of psychology lacks the resources required to account for such situations. It is no surprise that a folk theory that is incomplete, partial, and in many cases seriously defective often causes predictive failures. But this option is obviously not available for ST: simulation-driven predictions are "cognitively impenetrable," that is, they are not affected by the predictor's knowledge or ignorance about psychological processes (see also Saxe 2005; and the replies by Gordon 2005 and Goldman 2006: 173-4). More recently, however, a consensus seems to be emerging to the effect that mindreading involves both TT and ST. For example, Goldman (2006) grants a variety of possible roles for theorizing in the context of what he calls "high-level mindreading." This is the imaginative simulation discussed so far, which is subject to voluntary control, is accessible to consciousness, and involves the ascription of complex mental states such as propositional attitudes. High-level simulation is a species of what Goldman terms "enactment imagination" (a notion that builds on Currie & Ravenscroft's 2002 concept of "recreative imagination"). Goldman contrasts high-level mindreading to the "low-level mindreading," which is unconscious, hard-wired, involves the attribution of structurally simple mental states such as face-based emotions (for example, joy, fear, disgust), and relies on simple imitative or mirroring processes (see, for example, Goldman & Shripad 2005). Now, theory plays a role in high-level mindreading. In a prediction task, for example, theory may be involved in the selection of the imaginary inputs that will be introduced into the executive system. In this case, Goldman (2006: 44) admits, mindreading depends on the cooperation of simulation and theorizing mechanisms. Goldman's blend of ST and TT (albeit with a strong emphasis on the simulative component) is not the only "hybrid" account of mindreading: for other hybrid approaches, see Cotterill & Carruthers (1999), Nichols & Stich (2003), and Penner & Muhlberger (2006). And it is right to say that now the debate aims first to establish to what extent and in which processes theory or simulation prevails. a. Simulation with and without Introspection There is an aspect, however, that makes Goldman's (2006) account of ST different from other hybrid theories of mindreading, namely the neo-Cartesian priority that he assigns to introspection. On his view, first-person mindreading both ontogenetically precedes and grounds third-person mindreading. Mind readers need to introspectively access their offline products of simulation before they can project them onto the target. And this, Goldman claims, is a form of "direct access." In 1993 Goldman put forward a phenomenological version of the inside access view (see above, §1c), by arguing that introspection is a process of detection and classification of one's (current) psychological states that does not depend at all on theoretical knowledge, but rather occurs in virtue of information about the phenomenological properties of such states. But considering criticism (Carruthers 1996; Nichols & Stich 2003), in his 2006 book Goldman has remarkably reappraised the relevance of the qualitative component for the detection of psychological states, pointing out the centrality of the neural properties. Building on Craig's (2002) account of interception, as well as Marr's and Biederman's computational models of visual object recognition, Goldman now maintains that introspection is a perception-like process that involves a transduction mechanism that takes neural properties of mental states as input and outputs representations in a proprietary code (the introspective code, or the "I-code"). The I-code represents types of mental categories and classifies mental-state tokens in terms of those categories. Goldman also suggests some possible primitives of the I-code. So, for example, our coding of the concept of pain might be the combination of the "bodily feeling" parameter (a certain raw feeling) with the "preference" or "valence" one (a negative valence toward the feeling). Thus, the neural version of the inside access view is an attempt to solve the problem of the recognition of the attitude type, which proved problematic for Nichols and Stich's representationalism-functionalist approach (see above, §1c). However, since different percept and attitude types are presumably realized in different cerebral areas, each percept or attitude type will depend on a specific informational channel to feed the introspective mechanism. Consequently, Goldman's theory also seems to be open to the objection of massive disposability raised to the MM theory (see Engelbart and Carruthers 2010: 247). Goldman's primacy of first-person mindreading is, however, rejected by other situationists. According to Gordon's (1995, 1996) "radical" version of ST, simulation can occur without introspective access to one's own mental states. The simulative process begins not with my pretending to be the target, but rather with my becoming the target. As Gordon (1995: 54) puts it, simulation is not "a transfer but a transformation." "I" changes its referent and the equivalence "I=target" is established. In virtue of this de-rigidification of the personal pronoun, any introspective step is ruled out: one does not first assign a psychological state to oneself to transfer it to the target. Since the simulator becomes the target, no analogical inference from oneself to the other is needed. Still more radically, simulation can occur without having any mentalistic concepts. Our basic competence in the use of utterances of the form "I <propositional attitude> that p" involves not direct access to the propositional attitudes, but only an "ascent routine" through which we express our propositional attitudes in this new linguistic form (see Gordon 2007). Carruthers has raised two objections to Gordon's radical ST. First, it is a "step back" to a form of "quasi-behaviourism" (Carruthers 1996: 38). Second, Gordon problematically assumes that our mentalistic abilities are constituted by language (Carruthers 2011: 225-27). In developmental psychology de Villiers & de Villiers (2003) have put forward a constitution-thesis like Gordon's: thinking about mental states comes from internalizing the language with which these states are expressed in the child's linguistic environment. More specifically, mastery of the grammatical rules for embedding tensed complement clauses under verbs of speech or cognition provides children with a necessary representational format for dealing with false beliefs. However, correlation between linguistic exposure and mindreading does not depend on the use of specific grammatical structures. In a training study Lohman & Tomaselli (2003) found that performance on a false-belief task is enhanced by simply using perspective-shifting discourse, without any use of sentential complement syntax. Moreover, syntax is not constitutive of the mentalistic capacities of adults. Varley et al. (2001) and Dapperly et al. (2006) provided clear evidence that adults with profound grammatical impairment show no impairments on non-verbal tests of mindreading. Finally, mastery of sentence complements is not even a necessary condition of the development of mindreading in children. Penner et al. (2005) have shown that such mastery may be required for statements about beliefs but not about desires (as in English), for beliefs and desires (as in German), or for neither beliefs nor desires (Chinese); and yet children who learn each of these three languages all understand and talk about desire significantly earlier than belief.

b. Simulation in Low-Level Mindreading Another argument for a (prevalently) simulations approach to mindreading consists in pointing out that TT is thoroughly limited to high-level mindreading (essentially the attribution of propositional attitudes), whereas ST is also well equipped to account for forms of low-level mindreading such as the perception of emotions or the recognition of facial expressions and motor intentions (see Slurs & Macdonald 2008: 155).

This claim finds its main support in the interplay between ST and neuroscience. In the early 1990s mirror neurons were first described in the ventral premotor cortex and inferior parietal lobe of macaque monkeys. These visuomotor neurons activate not only when the monkey executes motor acts (such as grasping, manipulating, holding, and tearing objects), but also when it observes the same, or similar, acts performed by the experimenter or a conspecific. Although there is only one study that seems to offer direct evidence for the existence of mirror neurons in humans (Mikael et al. 2010), many neurophysiological and brain imaging investigations support the existence of a human action mirroring system. For example, fMRI studies using action observation or imitation tasks demonstrated activation in areas in the human ventral premotor and parietal cortices assumed to be homologous to the areas in the monkey cortex containing mirror neurons (see Pizzolatto et al. 2002). It should be emphasized that most of the mirror neurons that discharge when a certain type of motor act is performed also activate when the same act is perceived, even though it is not performed with the same physical movement—for example, many mirror neurons that discharge when the monkey grasps food with the hand also activate when it sees a conspecific who grasps food with the mouth. This seems to suggest that mirror neurons code or represent an action at a high level of abstraction, that is, they are receptive not only to a mere movement but indeed to an action. In 1998, Vittorio Gales and Goldman wrote a very influential article in which mirror neurons were indicated as the basis of the simulative process. When the mirror neurons in the simulator's brain are externally activated in observation mode, their activity matches (simulates or resonates with) that of mirror neurons in the target's brain, and this resonance process reproductively outputs a representation of the target's intention from a perception of her movement. More recently several objections have been raised against the "resonance" ST advocated by some researchers that have built on Gales and Goldman's hypothesis. Some critics, although admitting the presence of mirror neurons in both non-human and human primates, have drastically reappraised their role in mindreading. For example, Saxe (2009) has argued that there is no evidence that mirror neurons represent the internal states of the target rather than some relatively abstract properties of observed actions (see also Jacob & Jeanne rod 2005; Jacob 2008). On the other hand, Goldman himself has mitigated his original position. Unlike Gales, Keysets & Pizzolatto (2004), who propose mirror systems as the unifying basis of all social cognition, now Goldman (2006) considers mirror neuron activity, or motor resonance in general, as merely a possible part of low-level mindreading. Nonetheless, it is right to say that resonance phenomena are at the forefront of the field of social neuroscience (see Slurs & Macdonald 2008: 156).

3. Social Cognition without Mindreading

By the early 21st century, the primacy that both TT and ST assigns to mindreading in social cognition had been challenged. One line of attack has come from philosophers working in the phenomenological tradition, such as Shaun Gallagher, Matthew Ratcliffe, and Dan Zehavi (see Gallagher & Zehavi 2008). Others working more from the analytic tradition, such as Jose Luis Bermudez (2005, 2006b), Dan Hutto (2008), and Heidi Meibum (2003, 2007) have made similar points. Let's focus on Bermudez' contribution because he offers a very clear account of the kind of cognitive mechanisms that might sub serve forms of social understanding and coordination without mindreading (for a brief overview of this literature, see Slurs & Macdonald 2008; for an exhaustive examination, see Hersch Bach 2010).

Bermudez (2005) argues that the role of high-level mindreading in social cognition needs to be drastically re-evaluated. We must rethink the traditional nexus between intelligent behaviour and propositional attitudes, realizing that much social understanding and social coordination are sub served by mechanisms that do not capitalize on the machinery of intentional psychology. For example, a mechanism of emotional sensitivity such as "social referencing" is a form of low-level mindreading that sub serve social understanding and social coordination without involving the attribution of propositional attitudes (see Bermudez 2006a: 55). To this point Bermudez is on the same wavelength as situationists and social neuroscientists in drawing our attention to forms of low-level mindreading that have been largely neglected by philosophers. However, Bermudez goes a step beyond them and explores cases of social interactions that point in a different direction, that is, situations that involve mechanisms that can no longer be described as mindreading mechanisms. He offers two examples.

(1) In game theory there are social interactions that are modelled without assuming that the agents involved are engaged in explaining or predicting each other's behaviour. In social situations that have the structure of the iterated prisoner's dilemma, the so-called "tit-for-tat" heuristic simply says: "start out cooperating and then mirror your partner's move for each successive move" (Axelrod 1984). Applying this heuristic simply requires understanding the moves available to each player (cooperation or defection) and remembering what happened in

the last round. So, we have here a case of social interaction that is conducted based on a heuristic strategy that looks backward to the results of previous interactions rather than to their psychological ethology. We do not need to infer other players' reasons; we only must coordinate our behaviour with theirs. (2) There is another important class of social interactions that involve our predicting and/or explaining the actions of other participants, but in which the relevant predictions and explanations seem to proceed without us having to attribute propositional attitudes. These social interactions rest on what social psychologists call "scripts" ("frames" in artificial intelligence), that is, complex information structures that allow predictions to be made on the basis of the specification of the purpose of some social practice (for example, eating a meal at a restaurant), the various individual roles, and the appropriate sequence of moves. According to Bermudez, then, much social interaction is enabled by a suite of relatively simple mechanisms that exploit purely behavioural regularities. It is important to notice that these mechanisms sub serve central social cognition (in Feodor's sense). Nevertheless, they implement relatively simple processes of template matching and pattern recognition, that is, processes that are paradigmatic cases of perceptual processing. For example, when a player A applies the tit-for-tat rule, A must determine what the other player B did in the preceding round. This can be implemented in virtue of a template matching in which A verifies that B's behavioural pattern matches A's prototype of cooperation and defection. And also detecting the social roles implicated in a script-based interaction is a case of template matching: one verifies whether the perceived behaviour matches one of the templates associated with the script (or the prototype represented in the "frame"). Bermudez (2005: 223) notes that the idea that much of what we intuitively identify as central processing is actually implemented by mechanisms of template matching and pattern recognition has been repeatedly put forward by the advocates of the connectionist computationalism, especially by Paul M. Churchland. But unlike the latter, Bermudez does not carry the reappraisal of the role of propositional attitudes in social cognition to the point of their elimination; he argues that social cognition does not involve high-level mindreading when the social world is "transparent" or "ready-to-hand," as he says quoting Heidegger's zander. However, when we find ourselves in social situations that are "opaque," that is, situations in which all the standard mechanisms of social understanding and interpersonal negotiation break down, it seems that we cannot help but appeal to the type of metarepresentational thinking characteristic of intentional psychology (2005: 205-6).

Meaning of Human Mind:

Human Mind is the sum-total of various mental processes such as observing, knowing, thinking, reasoning, feeling, wishing, imagining, remembering, judging and others. It is not a separate object which has or possesses these mental processes. Mind is these mental processes. If we take away these mental processes. No mind is left, just as no chair is left if we take away its back, seat, arms, and legs. Therefore, mind is another name for those mental processes and activities put together.

Our Human mind grows just as our body grows. It becomes more complex with advancing years. In other words, our mental processes become richer and more complicated day by day. For example, there is a difference between thinking and reasoning of an adult and those of a child of three years. The human mind is not only the sum-total of all conscious mental processes, as it was believed earlier; it includes preconscious and unconscious processes, as well. It must be noted, however, that mind is one and is a unity. There are three levels at which it functions. At one level, we are aware of our mental processes; this is the 'conscious'.

At another level, we are not conscious of our mental processes; this gives us the "unconscious', still at another level, we are not aware of our mental processes at a certain time, but we were aware of them before, and can, again, be aware of them if we try. This is our preconscious.

The Unconscious:

The unconscious processes constitute the unconscious or the unconscious mind. It is the processes of which we are incapable of becoming conscious unless special methods of psychoanalysis are used. These processes lie buried deep down in the hidden recesses of our mind, very much below the level of consciousness.

It was Freud and his earliest followers Jung and Adler who strongly advocated the existence of the unconscious which could be understood and known through psycho-analysis – a method of unearthing and analysing the unconscious. Due to the discovery of the unconscious, our knowledge of the human mind is very much extended.

These thinkers have told us that the unconscious includes all forgotten past experiences, our repressed wishes and desires, our fears, and phobias for which we do not know the reason, or our eccentric likes and dislikes. Many of these unconscious mental processes appear in and cause our dreams, slips of pen or tongue. They cause abnormal behaviour in the form of neuroses and psychoses.

It must be noted that there are no pigeon-holes or compartments in our mind which store the pre-conscious or unconscious processes separately. The preconscious and unconscious are a part of the same mind to which the conscious processes belong. The former are simply those mental processes which we have forgotten, either temporarily or permanently. Their connections with our conscious process are broken for the time being.

These are as follows:

(I) Freud refers to the unconscious, the preconscious and the conscious as the topographical aspects of the mind or self or psyche. For him, the unconscious is of paramount importance. It is the true psychic reality. The conscious is only a fraction when compared with the vast unconscious. In it are stored and found millions of infantile wishes, unsatisfied desires, cravings, and urges, many of which are legacies from childhood.

Freud proves the existence of the unconscious by referring to many phenomena such as our experiences that we cannot recall, the phenomenon of somnambulism, post-hypnotic suggestion, dreams, morbid forgetfulness and slips of pen and tongue.

(ii) The second tenet of this system is the dynamic aspects of mind the — Id, the Ego, and the Super ego. Freud believed that all behaviour is the resultant of the dynamic conflicts between the forces of the Id, the Ego, and the Superego at the conscious, and unconscious levels of mind. The Id is the primitive undifferentiated basis of the whole human mind. It is completely dominated by the pleasure principle. It has no idea of time or reality. Its strivings are originally impulsive and uncontrolled out they are controlled by society and the reality principle during development.

The Ego represents the self or the conscious intelligence. It is the integrating part of the personality. It is an adjuster between the wishes of the Id on the one hand and the demands of external reality on the other. It must face the three sets of forces e.g., external reality, the instinctive pressure from the Id and inhibition or control from the Superego.

The Superego is the chief force that makes for the socialisation of the individual. It is primarily sociologically and culturally conditioned. It corresponds to the idea of conscience. It represents the social and moral ideal which society sets up for our behaviour. Within it reside the forces of repression and censorship, self-observation, and self-criticism. Mitchell says, 'By means of identification with the parents or one of the parents and Ego-ideal is set up within the Ego, and as a Superego, adopts and critical and condemnatory attitude of the parents towards the libidinal impulses.

(iii) The third tenet of psychoanalysis is that of conflict, repression, and complexes. As said above, according to Freud, all behaviour is the resultant of the dynamic conflicts between the forces of the Id, the Ego, and the Super-ego. The Id impulses which are largely sexual and aggressive in nature want to be satisfied, but these come in conflict with the Ego and the Super-ego. In other words, there is a clash between the primitive impulses and social and moral taboos, prohibitions, and obstructions. Our conflicts may be conscious or unconscious. When we are aware of the conflict and sources causing it, the conflict is at the conscious level. But there are times when we are not aware of the real motives causing conflict. We experience feelings of strain, stress, and anxiety but why? We cannot easily tell. The motivations of the conflict are unconscious. We are not aware of them. This is the end psychic or unconscious conflict.

This is how it happens. The conflict even at the conscious level, is a painful affair which creates tension in the human mind. It should end as soon as possible. It can be ended by following the Id impulses and by ignoring the claims of the Ego and the Super-ego or the external world. It can be ended by consciously denying the impulses or urges completely and following the demands of the Ego or Super-ego.

Another method of ending the conflicts is by throwing those impulses into allied channels sanctioned by society and thus obtaining for them a vicarious satisfaction. For example, many women who do not marry, satisfy a fundamental wish by becoming nurses or by directing their own energies to the care and welfare of children. But most people follow neither of these courses, it is very difficult to endure the ideas of defeat which result from the denial or our Id, desires.

Again, the Id impulses cannot be satisfied in the face of social opposition. Even throwing them into other social sanctioned channels is not an easy task. We need suitable potentialities, education, guidance, and environment for that. Normally, the conflict is resolved or ended, in an average individual, by an actual forcing down of these wishes into the unconscious.

This unconscious forgetfulness of the Id impulses or throwing down of these impulses into the unconscious is called repression. Thus, "what is unpleasant obnoxious, embarrassing or offensive is vanished from consciousness". With repression, the conflict shifts from the conscious into the unconscious.

These repressed wishes or desires remain active in the unconscious regions of our mind. They slowly gather strength by making alliance with other allied repressed experiences, thus forming an active group. This group of repressed desires working with a common end, i.e. to come back to the level of consciousness, is called a complex. As soon as complexes are formed, they give rise to a conflict in the unconscious, known as the endocyclic conflict. These complexes are just like exiles whose presence back in the conscious is not tolerated. But they do strive to regain consciousness. The forces of the Ego and Super-ego would not permit this. If they come back to the conscious, they would again create conflict and tension.

The mental force that keeps the repressed undesirable wishes confined to the unconscious is technically known as the censor. The censor is not an outside agency implanted in us but is a part of our own personality. It represents the moral and social aspects of the Ego and Super-ego.

But the censor is always not uniformly vigilant, its activities are considerably weakened during sleep as also during such moments that the repressed wishes seek to regain consciousness. At times, they may come in mask or in disguise and thus elude the vigilance of the censor. Such disguise may take the form of dreams, slips of pen and tongue, forgetfulness, mannerism of speech and others.

Sometimes, they may manifest themselves in mental mechanisms such as transference, projection identification, rationalization, and others. The complexes may also cause neurotic disturbances or psychotic disorders of various types.

(iv) The fourth principle of psychoanalysis is Freud's theory of instinct and libido. According to him, there are two decidedly inmates' psychological urges or instincts. These urges may be called 'Eros' of life or love instinct and Thanatos or the death instincts or aggression. They work through the existing structure of a person's being in his environment and determine what he is and what he does.

They are modified by the life experience of the individual, particularly those of the earliest years of life. These instincts are not opposed and mutually independent forces. They fuse and intermix. The intermixture of the two instincts leads to the Freudian principle of ambivalence loving and hating the same person.

Libido is the energy that works throughout the whole psychic system the energy of the life instinct. It is the source of sexual love, self-love, parental affection, friendship and of love for humanity in general. It causes the infantile sex-life; when the libido flows outward, it causes object-love; when it flows inward, it causes self-love or narcissism.

(v) The fifth tenet of the psycho-analytical theory is the principle of psycho- sexual genesis or infantile sexuality. Sexual life, according to Freud, does not start at puberty. Its first manifestations may be clearly seen after birth. Sexuality embraces many activities which have no connection with genitals. The fundamental functions of sexuality are to obtain pleasure from zones of the body. During the infancy and childhood period, this sexuality has three phases (a) oral, (b) anal-sadistic and (c) phallic.

At first the child derives libidinal satisfaction from the mouth; at three or four this pleasure is given by anal movement. After this we have the phallic phase when the child evinces interest in his genitalia. It is in this phase when the development of the Oedipus Complex takes place. The libido is directed towards an external love object of the opposite sex.

The latency period (5 to 12 years) is essentially one of psychic consolidation and synthesis. The psyche has a respite from infantile urges and the Super-ego develops. The pubertal period extends from 12 years onwards. There is a revival of sexuality and its passes through auto-erotic and homosexual phases before it is allowed its normal outlet in heterosexual behaviour.

Meaning of Human Mind:

Human Mind is the sum-total of various mental processes such as observing, knowing, thinking, reasoning, feeling, wishing, imagining, remembering, judging and others. It is not a separate object which has or possesses these mental processes. Mind is these mental processes. If we take away these mental processes. No mind is left, just as no chair is left if we take away its back, seat, arms, and legs. Therefore, mind is another name for those mental processes and activities put together. Our Human mind grows just as our body grows. It becomes more complex with advancing years. In other words, our mental processes become richer and more complicated day by day. For example, there is a difference between thinking and reasoning of an adult and those of a child of three years. The human mind is not only the sum-total of all conscious mental processes, as it was believed earlier; it includes preconscious and unconscious processes, as well. It must be noted, however, that mind is one and is a unity. There are three levels at which it functions. At one level, we are aware of our mental processes; this is the 'conscious'. At another level, we are not conscious of our mental processes; this gives us the "unconscious', still at another level, we are not aware of our mental processes at a certain time, but we were aware of them before, and can, again, be aware of them if we try. This is our preconscious. The Unconscious:

The unconscious processes constitute the unconscious or the unconscious mind. It is the processes of which we are incapable of becoming conscious unless special methods of psychoanalysis are used. These processes lie buried deep down in the hidden recesses of our mind, very much below the level of consciousness. It was Freud and his earliest followers Jung and Adler who strongly advocated the existence of the unconscious which could be understood and known through psycho-analysis – a method of unearthing and analysing the unconscious. Due to the discovery of the unconscious, our knowledge of the human mind is very much extended. These thinkers have told us that the unconscious includes all forgotten past experiences, our repressed wishes and desires, our fears, and phobias for which we do not know the reason, or our eccentric likes and dislikes. Many of these unconscious mental processes appear in and cause our dreams, slips of pen or tongue. They cause abnormal behaviour in the form of neuroses and psychoses. It must be noted that there are no pigeon-holes or compartments in our mind which store the pre-conscious or unconscious processes separately. The preconscious and unconscious are a part of the same mind to which the conscious processes belong. The former are simply those mental processes which we have forgotten, either temporarily or permanently. Their connections with our conscious process are broken for the time being.

These are as follows: (I) Freud refers to the unconscious, the preconscious and the conscious as the topographical aspects of the mind or self or psyche. For him, the unconscious is of paramount importance. It is the true psychic reality. The conscious is only a fraction when compared with the vast unconscious. In it are stored and found millions of infantile wishes, unsatisfied desires, cravings, and urges, many of which are legacies from childhood. Freud proves the existence of the unconscious by referring to many phenomena such as our experiences that we cannot recall, the phenomenon of somnambulism, post-hypnotic suggestion, dreams, morbid forgetfulness and slips of pen and tongue. (ii) The second tenet of this system is the dynamic aspects of mind the – Id, the Ego, and the Super ego. Freud believed that all behaviour is the resultant of the dynamic conflicts between the forces of the Id, the Ego, and the Superego at the conscious, and unconscious levels of mind. The Id is the primitive undifferentiated basis of the whole human mind. It is completely dominated by the pleasure principle. It has no idea of time or reality. Its strivings are originally impulsive and uncontrolled out they are controlled by society and the reality principle during development. Structure of the Mind the Ego represents the self or the conscious intelligence. It is the integrating part of the personality. It is an adjuster between the wishes of the Id on the one hand and the demands of external reality on the other. It must face the three sets of forces e.g., external reality, the instinctive pressure from the Id and inhibition or control from the Superego. The Superego is the chief force that makes for the socialisation of the individual. It is primarily sociologically and culturally conditioned. It corresponds to the idea of conscience. It represents the social and moral ideal which society sets up for our behaviour. Within it reside the forces of repression and censorship, self-observation, and self-criticism. Mitchell says, 'By means of identification with the parents or one of the parents and Ego-ideal is set up within the Ego, and as a Superego, adopts and critical and condemnatory attitude of the parents towards the libidinal impulses. (iii) The third tenet of psychoanalysis is that of conflict, repression, and complexes. As said above, according to Freud, all behaviour is the resultant of the dynamic conflicts between the forces of the Id, the Ego, and the Super-ego. The Id impulses which are largely sexual and aggressive in nature want to be satisfied, but these come in conflict with the Ego and the Super-ego. In other words, there is a clash between the primitive impulses and social and moral taboos, prohibitions, and obstructions. Our conflicts may be conscious or unconscious. When we are aware of the conflict and sources causing it, the conflict is at the conscious level. But there are times when we are not aware of the real motives causing conflict. We experience feelings of strain, stress, and anxiety but why? We cannot easily tell. The motivations of the conflict are unconscious. We are not aware of them. This is the end psychic or unconscious conflict. This is how it happens. The conflict even at the conscious level, is a painful affair which creates tension in the human mind. It should end as soon as possible. It can be ended by following the Id impulses and by ignoring the claims of the Ego and the Super-ego or the external world. It can be ended by consciously denying the impulses or urges completely and following the demands of the Ego or Super-ego. Another method of ending the conflicts is by throwing those impulses into allied channels sanctioned by society and thus obtaining for them a vicarious satisfaction. For example, many women who do not marry, satisfy a fundamental wish by becoming nurses or by directing their own energies to the care and welfare of children. But most people follow neither of these courses, it is very difficult to endure the ideas of defeat which result from the denial or our Id, desires. Again, the Id impulses cannot be satisfied in the face of social opposition. Even throwing them into other social sanctioned channels is not an easy task. We need suitable potentialities, education, guidance, and environment for that. Normally, the conflict is resolved or ended, in an average individual, by an actual forcing down of these wishes into the unconscious. This unconscious forgetfulness of the Id impulses or throwing down of these impulses into the unconscious is called repression. Thus, "what is unpleasant obnoxious, embarrassing or offensive is vanished from consciousness". With repression, the conflict shifts from the conscious into the unconscious. These repressed wishes or desires remain active in the unconscious regions of our mind. They slowly gather strength by making alliance with other allied repressed experiences, thus forming an active group. This group of repressed desires working with a common end, i.e. to come back to the level of consciousness, is called a complex. As soon as complexes are formed, they give rise to a conflict in the unconscious, known as the endocyclic conflict. Structure of the Human Mind Compared to an Iceberg These complexes are just like exiles whose presence back in the conscious is not tolerated. But they do strive to regain consciousness. The forces of the Ego and Super-ego would not permit this. If they come back to the conscious, they would again create conflict and tension. The mental force that keeps the repressed undesirable wishes confined to the unconscious is technically known as the censor. The censor is not an outside agency implanted in us but is a part of our own personality. It represents the moral and social aspects of the Ego and Super-ego. But the censor is always not uniformly vigilant, its activities are considerably weakened during sleep as also during such moments that the repressed wishes seek to regain consciousness. At times, they may come in mask or in disguise and thus elude the vigilance of the censor. Such disguise may take the form of dreams, slips of pen and tongue, forgetfulness, mannerism of speech and others. Sometimes, they may manifest themselves in mental mechanisms such as transference, projection identification, rationalization, and others. The complexes may also cause neurotic disturbances or psychotic disorders of various types. (iv) The fourth principle of psychoanalysis is Freud's theory of instinct and libido. According to him, there are two decidedly inmates' psychological urges or instincts. These urges may be called 'Eros' of life or love instinct and Thanatos or the death instincts or aggression. They work through the existing structure of a person's being in his environment and determine what he is and what he does. They are modified by the life experience of the individual, particularly those of the earliest years of life. These instincts are not opposed and mutually independent forces. They fuse and intermix. The intermixture of the two instincts leads to the Freudian principle of ambivalence loving and hating the same person. Libido is the energy that works throughout the whole psychic system the energy of the life instinct. It is the source of sexual love, self-love, parental affection, friendship and of love for humanity in general. It causes the infantile sex-life; when the libido flows outward, it causes object-love; when it flows inward, it causes self-love or narcissism. (v) The fifth tenet of the psycho-analytical theory is the principle of psycho- sexual genesis or infantile sexuality. Sexual life, according to Freud, does not start at puberty. Its first manifestations may be clearly seen after birth. Sexuality embraces many activities which have no connection with genitals. The fundamental functions of sexuality are to obtain pleasure from zones of the body. During the infancy and childhood period, this sexuality has three phases (a) oral, (b) anal-sadistic and (c) phallic. At first the child derives libidinal satisfaction from the mouth; at three or four this pleasure is given by anal movement.

After this we have the phallic phase when the child evinces interest in his genitalia. It is in this phase when the development of the Oedipus Complex takes place. The libido is directed towards an external love object of the opposite sex. The latency period (5 to 12 years) is essentially one of psychic consolidation and synthesis. The psyche has a respite from infantile urges and the Super-ego develops. The pubertal period extends from 12 years onwards. There is a revival of sexuality and its passes through auto-erotic and homosexual phases before it is allowed its normal outlet in heterosexual behaviour. Mind power is one of the strongest and most useful powers you possess.

This power consists of your thoughts.

The thoughts that pass through your mind are responsible for everything that happens in your life. Your predominant thoughts influence your behaviour and attitude and control your actions and reactions. As your thoughts are, so is your life. Be careful of what you think

Thoughts are like a video that plays on the screen of your mind. What you play there, determines the kind of life you live and the experiences you meet. To make changes in your life, you must play a different video, one that you like more. The Power of Thoughts Is a Creative Power

You can train and strengthen this power. You can use it to make changes in your life, and to influence other people's minds. If you plant seeds, water them, and give them fertilizers, they will grow into healthy and strong plants. Thoughts, like seeds, have a natural tendency to grow and manifest in your life, if you feed them with attention, interest, and enthusiasm. Your thoughts pass from your conscious mind to your subconscious mind, which in turn, influences your actions in accordance with these thoughts. Your thoughts also pass to other minds, and consequently, people who can help you, might offer you their help, sometimes, without even knowing why. This might some strange and unbelievable. You don't have to accept these words, but if you analyse the kind of thoughts you think, and the kind of life you live, you will discover interesting things about the mind. The power of your mind is part of the creative power of the Universe, which means that your thoughts work together with it. You are a manifestation of the Universal mind. When you repeat the same thought over and again, in one way or another, this mighty power helps you make your thoughts come true. Using the power of thoughts effectively, is an act of "practical daydreaming". How to Use the Power of Your Thoughts? Visualize a perfect scene of whatever you want to accomplish.

Put a lot of detail, colour, sound, scent, and life into these mental scenes.

Repeat your visualization often, with faith and attention, and your subconscious will accept these mental scenes as real experiences. The subconscious mind does not distinguish between real and imaginary experiences and accepts both as real. It will start making changes and attracting opportunities, to make your reality match the images in your subconscious mind.

Actions, situations, and objects that you visualize frequently, eventually, manifest on the material plane in a natural way. This manifestation does not happen overnight. It needs time, and depends on how ambitious and sincere you are, and how much time and attention you put into this action. You can use this process to change negative habits and build new, positive habits or skills. You can also use it for attracting money and possessions, for promotion at work, for building a business, improving health and relationships, changing circumstances, and for practically almost everything. Pay attention to the thoughts you think. Do your best to reject negative thoughts, and to allow into your mind only thoughts that bring good, happy, and positive results.

The good news is that there are a number of different ways to improve your brain power, especially if you're willing to do some things consistently over a longer period of time. Let's explore eight ways that you can support your brain health.

1. Exercise.

We all know that we should be getting regular exercise. However, most entrepreneur lead busy, rushed lives, and can't always find the time to fit physical activity in. The trick might be to think of it in reverse: you can't afford not to exercise if you want to live a long, healthy, productive life. Exercise not only benefits your brain health and cognition; it can also improve your memory. In the long run, it can even protect your brain against degeneration. If that isn't reason enough to get into a regular workout routine, who knows what is? Related: Why Food, Sleep and Exercise Are Critical to Success 2. Drink coffee.

Many people start their days with a cup of coffee, and it turns out this ritual could benefit your cognitive functions in the short term. Caffeine, of course, helps to keep you alert. However, it can also help you to stay focused on repetitive and tedious tasks, and will even boost your intelligence, including your reaction time and reasoning. Obviously, the effects of coffee are not permanent. However, it can make your brain work more efficiently until that caffeine high wears off. 3. Get some sunlight.

Sunlight and exercise can sometimes go hand in hand. This mostly depends on what part of the world you live in; how much sunlight is available at different times of the year and how realistic it is for you to spend time in the outdoors. Getting too little sunlight is not good for your brain. Higher levels of vitamin D in your system allow you to perform better and can even slow down the aging of your brain. Too much sunlight can be bad for your skin, but if you aren't getting enough, your brain functions may suffer. Of course, you can always take vitamin D supplements if you find that you aren't able to get outside as much as you would like to. Just remember to take supplements in moderation.4. Build strong connections. It has often been said that the entrepreneurial journey is a lonely one. As it turns out, that may not be good for your cognitive functions. If you often feel lonely, it can result in psychological and cognitive decline, as these feelings can have a negative impact on your sleep, increase your blood pressure, contribute to depression, and even lower your overall well-being. Most entrepreneurs know how to communicate and build connections. The key thing is to build a strong support system around you, as that will enable you to stay healthy mentally and psychologically over the long term. 5. Meditate.

Meditation is a trending topic among many entrepreneurs right now, and its benefits are hard to argue with. Not only does meditation reduce your stress levels, it can also prevent age-related disorders such as Alzheimer's or dementia. This speaks to the importance of self-care. Taking a mere 10 to 15 minutes out of your day to practice meditation could extend your cognitive longevity and allow you to reduce your overall stress levels too. Related: Less Sleep Makes You More Likely to Catch a Cold, Study Finds 6. Sleep well.

This can be another tricky area for entrepreneurs. Early mornings and late nights sometimes come with the territory, and the stresses or excitement that come with building and growing a business can have undesirable effects on sleep patterns. Sleep is required to consolidate memory and learning. If you don't get enough sleep, your Gray-matter volume in your frontal lobe may begin to decrease. Your frontal lobe supports and controls your working memory as well as executive function, making it particularly important. In short, if you don't get enough sleep, you'll have less brain in your head. 7. Eat well.

It shouldn't come as a surprise that nutrition plays a significant part in your brain health. Entrepreneurs are often rushing from one meeting to another, leaving themselves with very little or no time to eat well. You must focus on getting the right kind of nutrition. Antioxidants and amino acids are particularly important, and vitamin E can also be beneficial. Drinking wine is known to improve your cognitive function -- assuming you consume it in moderation -- and nuts, blueberries, whole grains, and avocados are also beneficial. What's good for your body also tends to be good for your brain. 8. Play Tetris. This might come to you as a bit of a surprise, but playing Tetris is known to have several positive effects on your brain. Playing Tetris will increase Gray matter for a short amount of time, and it can also help with performing spatially related tasks. The most interesting part is that playing Tetris after a traumatic experience can prevent your brain from solidifying those memories. That means fewer flashbacks to negative memories over the long haul. If you always have a smartphone or tablet with you, then incorporating a little bit of Tetris into your day should prove to be straightforward. Just don't get carried away and forget to work, too! Final thoughts More than anything else, improving your brain power is about habits, and habits take time to build. The best approach is to focus on one or two things at a time. Giving your life a complete makeover is going to prove much more challenging, and the habits you attempt to develop may not stick. This is counterproductive.

Not only is balance hard to achieve, often it never is in the life of an entrepreneur. However, constant experimentation and tweaking will allow you to test things out and see what works best for you. Have you ever had a fellow motorist stopped beside you at a red light, singing his brains out, or picking his nose, or otherwise behaving in ways he might not normally do in public? There is something about being alone in a car that encourages people to zone out and forget that others can see them. Although these little lapses of attention are amusing for the rest of us, they are also instructive when it comes to the topic of consciousness.

Summery-

The mind and its phenomena of qualia and consciousness are non-material entities with information and information processing as their essence. They evolved into existence to help increase the survival chance of the species that possess them. Why do we have the mind, qualia, and consciousness as they are manifesting phenomenally as vision, sound, smell, emotion, thought, etc. that we can experience mentally why are we not like computers or robots, doing everything "in the dark", without those phenomenal manifestations occurring? The answer is because the mind, qualia, and consciousness that manifest phenomenally have additional physical effects from their phenomenal manifestations, and those effects help increase the survival chance of ourselves and our species. Therefore, the mind, qualia, and consciousness as they are — having phenomenal manifestations — evolved into existence to help us and our species survive better. How do those phenomenal manifestations, the seemingly non-physical manifestations — such as the vision of the red colour, the musical sound, and the happy emotion in our mind, occur from neural processes, which are just physical processes — how can physical processes give rise to those seemingly non-physical phenomenal manifestations? ... The answer is because some neural processes have neural signals that mean, in the neural language, phenomenal manifestations, when these signals are read in the neural system, they will be interpreted as phenomenal manifestations, and phenomenal manifestations naturally and inevitably occur in the neural system. This is how qualia and consciousness occur with all their phenomenal manifestations in the physical brain.

Quick proof ⟹ Qualia have physical effect

Quick proof ⟹ Qualia are neural signals

"The Basic Theory of the Mind" is a physical theory about the mind and its phenomena, such as qualia and consciousness. It also involves related matters including the hard problem of consciousness, the explanatory gap, variable qualia, p-zombies, and free will. This theory is a scientifically verifiable theory – it is based on physical evidence and provides experimentally testable predictions.

The Mind-

The mind is one thing that has always fascinated and puzzled us. It is the only thing that we can be certain of existing, yet, apparently, we do not know exactly what it is, how it occurs, and why it occurs. This is in contrast to things outside the mind, such as houses, cars, and even other people, which we cannot be certain that they really exist – they may be just illusions – yet, apparently, we know what they are, how they occur, and why they occur. What is more, the phenomena of qualia and consciousness, such as the red colour as it appears phenomenally red in our mind and our phenomenal conscious awareness and experience of that red colour, have always been baffling – what is their nature, how and why do they occur, and cannot there be just the mind without them? Fortunately, with centuries of studying these matters, first by philosophers and later also by neurologists, neuroscientists, and other scientists in related fields, we now have a wealth of scientific evidence and concepts that are complete enough to form a theory that can answer these great puzzles. The Basic Theory of the Mind -

Based on the wealth of scientific evidence and concepts, this theory has been formed. Its essence is as follows:

1. From the physical properties of the mind and those of the brain (the alive, processing brain), it can be concluded that the mind always occurs, exists, and functions with the brain and that

the brain always occurs, exists, and functions with the mind. Both never occur alone without the other. They are a unity. Each is the intrinsic, equivalent, but different (non-material vs material) aspect of this unity.

2. From the physical properties of the mind and those of the brain's information-processing processes, which are non-material processes, it can be concluded that the mind is the composite of the information-processing processes of the brain "What happens when we see, hear, and smell things around us, experience moods, think of various things, plan appropriate actions, and command our hands, lips, and body to move, if not information, information, and information are being processed. We are just informational entities, ever processing information and living on the informational side of the universe."

1. The mind is an information-processing entity. Because the mind is a composite of information-processing processes, it is an informational entity — a non-material entity that is composed of information and information processing, and because the information processing processes that form the mind are innumerable in number and involve information that ranges from simple to very advanced, the mind is an informational entity in a highly advanced form. And, because the mind is a non-material, informational entity, it is not a conventional physical entity (or mechanical entity) like mass, energy, or force; that is why it is so different from the conventional physical entities.

3. Qualia, the mental phenomena that appear phenomenally in our mind and that we can consciously experience, such as the vision of a house, the sound of a song, and the door of a rose in our mind, are physical phenomena. They are governed by physical laws and are physically predictable. 2. Qualia are mental phenomena that we can consciously experience in our mind.

Specifically, they are neural process associated physical phenomena.

[Quick proof $\Rightarrow$ Qualia are physical phenomena]

4. From the physical properties of qualia and those of special kinds of neural-process signalling pattern, which are neural information and non-material, it can be concluded that qualia are special kinds of neural-process signalling pattern.

"If we look around and consciously experience the visual qualia occurring right in front of us now, with the facts that our consciousness can experience the visual qualia and that the only things the consciousness neural process is capable of reading are signalling patterns of neural processes, it is inescapable to conclude that we are, in fact, experiencing the signalling patterns of neural processes!"

[Quick proof ⇒ Qualia are signalling patterns]

Because neural-process signalling patterns are neural information, qualia are special kinds of neural information — neural information in specialized forms that, when read by neural processes, are interpreted to be entities with phenomenal appearances or qualia that appear phenomenally in our mind signalling pattern and qualia and consciousness

3. When read by neural processes, a normal signalling pattern (A) for a visual perception of a house means "House", so the mind gets only the physical information of the house (such as its width, length, height, luminosity, and colours) but not the information of what the house looks like. But a special signalling pattern (B) for a visual perception of the same house means "House and what the house looks like"; consequently, a quale of the house naturally and inevitably occurs in the mind. Like the mind, qualia are non-material, informational entities, not mechanical entities. And this answers the hard problem of qualia and bridges the explanatory gap of how non-material phenomenal qualia can arise from material neural processes: non-material phenomenal qualia are neural signalling patterns, which always exist intrinsically in material neural processes — no novel, non-material entities arise or emerge from material neural processes to be qualia.

5. From the physical properties of consciousness and those of a special kind of re-entrant signalling state, which is the neural information of the consciousness neural process and is non-material, it can be concluded that consciousness is a special kind of re-entrant signalling state. Because a neural-process signalling state is neural information consciousness is a special kind of neural information — neural information in a specialized form that, when read by the consciousness neural process itself by the process of re-entrant signalling, is interpreted to be entities with phenomenal appearances or consciousness that appears phenomenally in our mind signalling state and consciousness

4. When read by the consciousness neural process by the process of re-entrant signalling, a special signalling state of a visual perception of a house means "conscious awareness and experience of what the house looks like"; consequently, phenomenal consciousness of the house naturally and inevitably occurs. Like the mind and qualia, consciousness is a non-material, informational entity, not a mechanical entity. And this answers the hard problem of

consciousness and bridges the explanatory gap of how non-material phenomenal consciousness can arise from the material consciousness neural process: non-material phenomenal consciousness is a signalling state that always exists intrinsically in the material consciousness neural process — no novel, non-material entity arises or emerges from the material consciousness neural process to be consciousness.

6. The fact that qualia and conscious awareness and conscious experiences of the qualia occur in only the final-stage sensory perception neural processes and the highest-level cognitive and executive neural processes, which are the latest-evolved neural processes, and never occur in the more primitive neural processes, such as the brainstem, cerebellum, and basal ganglia, or over the whole brain scattered, indicates that they are not randomly occurring phenomena but are evolved functions of the nervous system.

7. Because a neural process that performs a certain function (such as perceiving a vision) without qualia occurring and a neural process that performs that same function (such as perceiving a vision) with qualia occurring have different information in the processes, they have different signalling patterns (to convey different information). Therefore, they have different physical effects on other neural processes, at least from the different effects of different signalling patterns. Qualia thus have physical effects. signalling patterns Ans meanings

5. Different signalling patterns have different meanings and different effects Also, because we do have conscious awareness and conscious experiences of qualia, qualia must certainly induce the consciousness neural process to function to be consciously aware of and to consciously experience the qualia; therefore, because the consciousness neural process is a physical process, qualia cause changes in a physical process and thus have physical effects. Similarly, it can be concluded that consciousness (conscious awareness and conscious experiences) has physical effects. Therefore, qualia and consciousness are evolved neural functions that have physical effects.

8. Because a function requires resources in building, maintaining, and operating the function and may have some negative effects, if its overall effects do not help increase the survival chance of the animals that have the function, those animals and the function will likely become extinct in the evolutionary process. This is especially true for a major function in a critical organ as in the case of qualia and consciousness in the brain. The fact that qualia and consciousness still exist today indicates that they have been selected to remain in the evolutionary process. This means that their overall effects must help increase the survival chance of the species that have them. Qualia and consciousness, in the form that they are —

phenomenal qualia and phenomenal consciousness, or qualia and consciousness that appear phenomenally in our mind – thus are evolved functions to help increase the survival chance of the species, including humans, that have them. This is the scientific answer to the other part of the hard problem of consciousness: why does consciousness in the form of phenomenal consciousness occur in this universe? This is also the scientific answer to one of the most basic questions of our lives: why do "we" exist? In conclusion:

"We" – our mind, qualia, and consciousness – exist

to increase the survival chance of ourselves

... and our species.

"You" – your mind, qualia, and consciousness – exist

to increase the survival chance of yourself

... and your species.

Green Mind Theory: How Brain-Body-Behaviour Links into Natural and Social Environments for Healthy Habits by Jules Pretty 1 Orchidometer Rogerson 2, ORCID and Barton ORCID

School of Biological Sciences, University of Essex, Colchester CO4 3SQ, UK school of Sport, Rehabilitation and Exercise Sciences, University of Essex, Colchester CO4 3SQ, UK

Author to whom correspondence should be addressed. All authors contributed equally to this work. Int. J. Environ. Res. Public Health 2017, 14(7), 706.

We propose a Green Mind Theory (GMT) to link the human mind with the brain and body and connect the body into natural and social environments. The processes are reciprocal: environments shape bodies, brains, and minds; minds change body behaviours that shape the external environment. GMT offers routes to improved individual well-being whilst building towards greener economies. It builds upon research on green exercise and nature-based therapies and draws on understanding derived from neuroscience and brain plasticity, spiritual and wisdom traditions, the lifeways of original cultures, and material consumption behaviours. We set out a simple metaphor for brain function: a bottom brain stem that is fast-acting, involuntary, impulsive, and the driver of fight and flight behaviours; a top brain cortex that is slower, voluntary, the centre for learning, and the driver of rest and digest. The bottom brain reacts before thought and directs the sympathetic nervous system. The top brain is calming, directing the parasympathetic nervous system. Here, we call the top brain blue and the bottom brain red; too much red brain is bad for health. In modern high-consumption economies, life has often come to be lived on red alert. An over-active red mode impacts the gastrointestinal, immune, cardiovascular, and endocrine systems. We develop our knowledge of nature-based interventions and suggest a framework for the blue brain-red brain-green mind. We show how activities involving immersive-attention quieten internal chatter, how habits affect behaviours across the life course, how long habits take to be formed and hard-wired into daily practice, the role of place making, and finally how green minds could foster prosocial and greener economies. We conclude with observations on twelve research priorities and health interventions, and ten calls to action.

Keywords: green minds; green exercise; nature and health; healthy behaviours

1. Recent Findings from Research on Nature and Health We have undertaken over a decade of research into the contexts, effects, and outcomes of green exercise and nature-based interventions, showing in a wide variety of contexts that physical activity in the presence of nature improves health and well-being We have found no groups who have not benefitted: all ages, genders, ethnicities, and social classes respond positively to green exercise. We have shown that all-natural environments are beneficial: from urban parks to biodiversity-rich ones, from small local to large landscapes, and from domesticated gardens to the farmed and wild. We coined the phrase dose of nature to articulate that exposure to green exercise is analogous to a medical dose to the body, improving mental health We have shown that the deliberate therapeutic use of natural environments (e.g., gardens, allotments, care farms, and wild places) has both short and long term positive effects on groups under mental stress, including at-risk children and youth, refugees, probationers, dementia sufferers, office workers, and mental health patients. The natural environment is now understood to provide vital health services as well as other environmental services These health services include direct and indirect effects on physical and mental health, and reductions in the threats of pollution and disease vectors.

Further research has filled many gaps, exploring inner mechanisms, external social processes, interactions with place and behaviours across the life course. It has been shown that greener environments reducing social inequality and having particularly positive impacts on mental well-being, that physical labour in the home is important for health and longevity and that blue space (locations in sight of water) is as important as green: it is not the colour that matters, but the opportunity to behave in a way that improves well-being. A meta-analysis of nature connectivity and well-being has shown the more connected to nature a person is, the greater is their life satisfaction. At the same time, the design of human settlements and buildings influences human health suggesting that natural places can be thought of as healing places Typical urban settings are more discomforting, with metabolic and well-being consequences. Exposure to nature reduces internal stress markers and produces healthier cortisol profiles. Knowing is important too. knowledge of being treated (both dose of nature and drug medication) causes a release of endogenous opioids that are non-addictive: the placebo effect demonstrates the mechanisms for self-healing (of some conditions) Life course and longitudinal studies (e.g., Caerphilly men, Dunedin, Maudsley and Cambridge cohorts, Milwaukee nuns, Harvard alumni) have shown how choices on behaviours, consumption, and mental states directly affect health and well-being over many decades. These studies demonstrate the value of early interventions with children whose cognitive outcomes are improved when regularly exposed to activity in natural places (playgrounds, gardens, and woodlands).

We have calculated the annual health costs of seven lifestyle-related conditions in the U.K. (obesity, type 2 diabetes, loneliness, cardiovascular diseases, mental ill-health, dementias, and physical inactivity), all of which are influenced by a lack of physical activity, links to natural places, and links to community and people; annually these amount to around £180 billion. All these conditions are influenced by a lack of physical activity, links to natural places, and links to community and people, with annual health costs ranging from £8–105 billion (Table 1). This suggests that high levels of material consumption in affluent countries have not necessarily brought increased health and well-being for all; that consumption patterns in most countries of the world are converging on those typical to the affluent; and that new ways of living are required that emphasise non-material consumption if planetary and personal harm is to be avoided

Table 1. The annual costs of the health externalities arising from modern lifestyles, U.K.

Table

Many of the drivers of ill-health in Table 1 are behaviour- and lifestyle-related: too many calories consumed in food and drink, too little physical activity, and too little social engagement. Through a variety of interventions, there is now the prospect of the U.K. becoming virtually tobacco-free (<16% of the adult population now smoke tobacco, down from 50% in the mid-1970s). Yet the implementation of healthy food, activity, and engagement activities for whole populations seems impossible, despite advances on nudge tactics (a concept that involves positive reinforcement to achieve non-forced compliance) Social and economic environments do shape behaviours. Residents of London walk 292 miles per year; but rural people walk just 122 miles. Obesity afflicts 35% of adults in the U.S.; in Manhattan, where there are pavements and public transport, people walk more, and only 15% are obese. In the Japanese, Sardinian, and Costa Rican longevity hotspots, cultures encourage healthy and tasty foods, regular physical activity outdoors, social connections, and continued cognitive engagement. Individual choices do not arise from failures of free-will but are shaped by the interactions between the design of lived environments, transport systems, institutional inertia, advertising and corporate self-interest, and access to green space. Here, we explore how behaviours benefitting health can be adopted and encouraged. 2. Red Brain, Blue Brain, Green Mind

We are proposing a Green Mind Theory (GMT) that links the human mind with the brain and body and connects the body with natural and social environments. The processes are reciprocal: environments shape bodies, brains, and minds; minds change body behaviours that shape social interactions and natural capital. GMT offers opportunities for improving individual well-being whilst building towards greener and prosocial economies that could protect the planetary future. The empirical understanding of green minds derives from evidence on neuroscience and brain plasticity, from spiritual and wisdom traditions from mindfulness-related and talking therapies from green exercise activities in nature from the lifeways of indigenous groups and from material consumption behaviours and the potential emergence of green and prosocial economies

We outline how and why pathways of poor health can be engaged by surrounding natural and social environments in ways that promote reciprocal individual-society-natural well-being. Our concern is not to assume a comprehensive description of many complex brain-body interactions, nor to take a simple behaviourist model whereby well-being or happiness can appear to be guaranteed. Our desire is to use an emerging understanding of brain-body-behaviours to develop pathways and interventions for better health and well-being.

We propose a simple brain metaphor with levels representing different stages of mammal-hominid evolution The brain stem (bottom brain) is the oldest and contains survival functions: it is fast responding, involuntary, automatic, impulsive, driven by emotions, and is the executor for habits and routines. In the mid-brain, the limbic/sub-cortex system is the central region comprising the hippocampus, hypothalamus and thalamus, and amygdala: it is the centre for emotions, memory forming, and bonding. The top-brain cortex is the most recent, having expanded in size rapidly during the later stages of hominid evolution: it is slower, voluntary, able to learn and plan, make internal choices, and contains centres for the social abilities of empathy and language. The top brain is calming, drives the parasympathetic nervous system (PNS), and is characterised by rest-and-digest. The bottom brain is spiked into action by the amygdala, the sentinel for emotional meaning, which drives the sympathetic nervous system (SNS) via the hypothalamus pituitary adrenal axis (HPAA) and is characterised by fight-and-flight. We call the top brain blue, and the bottom brain red.

We use the term green mind to suggest an optimal mixed mode of mainly activated PNS, interest and excitement associated mild SNS stimulation, and the presence of only occasional SNS spikes for alarm response. A mix of blue and red is best for health and well-being. Too much red brain is detrimental for health. The key endogenous neurotransmitters, hormones, and peptide pathways are serotonin (key to sleep and mood); dopamine (aids approach, attention, and rewards, but when it falls it makes us feel unpleasant); norepinephrine (promotes alertness and arousal); acetylcholine (promotes wakefulness and learning); opioids (reduces pain and buffer stress); oxytocin (a key role in bonding and feelings of bliss); cortisol (stimulates amygdala and inhibits hippocampus); oestrogen (key in memory); and adrenalin (stress hormone). Our proposal for the greener mind centres on activities that bring immersion-attentiveness, so calming the mind. We will later show how these centres on the choice architecture for engagements with nature, with other people, and with craft-skill based activities. Green Mind Theory suggests that desirable fundamentals to well-being are in reach of everyone. Yet the negativity bias of the brain has become dominant in modern living. A summary of the key differences between the modern and green mind is shown in Table 2.

Table 2. Ten differences between mind typical of modern affluent culture and the green mind.

Table

3. The Brain's Negativity Bias and Causes of Suffering

It is plausible that natural selection has built a negativity bias into the brain-mind the amygdala responds immediately to alerts and succeeds by being over-responsive. In evolutionary history, to miss one threat meant death; to miss one positive signal was not necessarily critical. The brain-mind thus evolved fast-acting and over-responsive fight-flight as the default mode. There is no moderation to the amygdala. It is a binary responder: fully on or off and responding before thought. In hunter-gatherer-cultivator communities (the old economies: sites for millions of years of prior evolution, the blue brain mode tends to dominate the predator or poisonous snake was rare, threats from other hominid bands also scarce. By contrast, in modern affluent cultures dominated by material consumption and dashed hope, the red alert mode is regularly activated. Modern life appears to be lived on simmer reducing almost non-stop SNS-HPAA activation.

Repeated SNS-HPAA stimulation leads to an over-reactive amygdala, resulting in high anxiety and the continual shading of memories with fear and anxiety. The current world gradually looks and feels worse, as does the past. The hippocampus is worn down, and memories harder to retain. Cortisol further suppresses new neurons in the hippocampus. Too much SNS-HPAA has negative impacts on the gastrointestinal system (more ulcers, inflammatory bowel syndrome), on the immune system (more colds and flu, slower wound healing), on the cardiovascular system (hardened arteries), and on the endocrine system (producing type 2 diabetes) Stress manifested as conditions (e.g., post-traumatic stress disorder (PTSD), depression) and illness (e.g., cardio-vascular disease) manifests internally as accumulation over long time periods of gradually worsening internal responses to the same stressors. Over time, continuing red brain activity exacts a cost, accelerating disease mechanisms, especially CVD, and the atrophy of brain structures (especially the hippocampus). Repeated hits of stress can leave stress hormone levels continually high, with no recovery period.

Modern living is often characterised by cognitive overload, impulsive habits, and individual behaviours that have led to a new generation of health challenges Just as shortages of food—eras of never-quite-enough—were solved in the 1950s–1970s in affluent countries, so food over-consumption became a leading problem just as eras of challenging transport requiring high energy expenditure ended, so inactivity and sedentary behaviours became common health problems. With these have come increased anxiety, guilt, and stress in a cosy modern world, many have forgotten discomfort finding it easy to habituate over-eating or drinking, or a reliance on pharmaceutical interventions. In time, the habits evolve into pre-emptive strikes: promoting consumption before the anticipated discomfort. Some spiritual and wisdom traditions call the red alerts first arrows these are fired by the amygdala and cannot be avoided. The second arrows, comprising how we feel in response to the first, commonly result in feelings of unfairness, guilt, further fear, anger, upset, and anxiety. Sometimes second arrows arise from anxious expectation, even when there have been no first arrow Threat signals are effective precisely because they are unpleasant. They should be they make us suffer.

The first arrow threat alarm causes the amygdala to stimulate the thalamus, which sends norepinephrine to the brain stem (red brain). The SNS signals organs and muscles to ready for fight-flight, the hypothalamus now signalling the pituitary to instruct the adrenal glands to release adrenaline, cortisol, and epinephrine. The body is now on red alert, the epinephrine having increased heart rate and dilated pupils for more light, the cortisol suppressing the immune system and hippocampus. The executive control of the prefrontal cortex is switched off. Suffering arising from first arrows is thus embodied and works through the cascade of SNS and HPAA. Most of the time, we hardly notice this is happening.

Modern affluent countries contain lonelier people and have a growing number of adults living alone Lonely adults display elevated cortisol and epinephrine levels and have higher blood pressure; the more active SNS-HPAA results in poorer sleep and lower immune function; it accelerates physiological decline with age Further linking the brain with behaviour, individuals with smaller social networks tend to have a smaller amygdala and hippocampus: structures that play an important role in social behaviour The lonely are red brain dominant, and their lifespan is reduced. In modern living, first arrows have become more common, and together with second arrows have negative impacts on memory, general well-being, and habit forming. A strong blue brain can dampen second arrows.

4. Immersion and Attentiveness to Quiet the Chatter A green mind should have a healthy mix of brain states, with a predominance of calm blue. A range of different descriptors have been used to describe a state of mind that results in a temporary dampening of second arrows by building up the PNS: focus, attention, awareness, and immersion. There is clear evidence to show that activities that are immersive and involve focused attention are effective in improving well-being they cause instant physiological changes by reducing oxygen consumption, lowering heart rate and blood pressure, and increasing the release of serotonin and dopamine The importance of recovering the capacity to focus attention was first proposed by Kaplan and Kaplan leading to a growing understanding of the restorative benefits of nature A variety of stressors cause attention fatigue: Attention Restoration Theory showed how focused attention, with positive well-being outcomes, could be recovered or restored by engagement with a variety of environments, both natural and non-natural More recently, research on palatogenesis, the range of factors supporting health and well-being, has developed an understanding of how environments can both deplete and restore internal resources here, we suggest it is the immersion and activation of the PNS that is the key mechanism. Some environments are thus seen as restorative, as are some behaviours and activities. We know that immersive-attention is an element of some green exercise, arising

during walking, moderate running, and gardening during meditative activities such as yoga, tai chi, and mindfulness and during many craft and skill-based activities such as woodwork, painting, knitting, and needlework In some, exercise involves no more than sitting; in others, it is part of cultural events: community dancing and singing of sinning of Tibet, the haka of Māori in New Zealand, the chain dance of Faroe, the reamer of Iceland, the shadow puppetry of Indonesia, the ceremonial dances of American Indian tribes, and forest bathing in Japan Being highly attentive could have brought evolutionary advantage to hunter-gatherer-cultivators. Watchful awareness is central to the hunt; is vital for caring for plants and animals across the seasons; is critical to memory creation for sources of water and signals for weather events. Hunter-gatherer-cultivators spent large amounts of time waiting, observing keenly, and preparing and eating food. Yet in material cultures and economies where a life on automatic seems a modern malaise, millions actively choose opportunities for quiet and calm: watching sunsets, beach holidays, being with friends, and activities that require focus and take time to learn. A second feature of a brain dominated by second arrows is the endless chatter that originates in the verbal and language centres of the left prefrontal cortex. This chatter comprises the loops of internal voice that act as commentary on past events, future possibilities, and current concerns the autobiographical self runs loops of past and future and is often self-critical. Anxiety retunes memories of the past, gradually making them feel worse. Immersive-attentive activities are calming and take time. They activate the PNS, and increase neurone growth in the insula, hippocampus, and prefrontal cortex, particularly the left prefrontal cortex (PFC) where feelings of well-being reside. A steady release of dopamine is produced, increasing a sense of well-being. The PNS further decreases cortisol and strengthens the activity of the immune system. Immersive attentiveness can thus feel like a high vantage point, being on a hill looking down on the distant valley below, or on cliffs looking at the silent sea. When the green mind is quiet, the self is stilled. A wandering mind is an unhappy mind

5. Habits and Behaviours in the Life course

Planning and learning occur in the PFC, and as routines are automated so they are sent downwards to the mid and lower brains and tend to remain fixed unless brought back up for specific improvements. As we habituate a routine more, so the basal ganglia take over from the PFC and automate the routine, allowing us to pay less attention (and use up less energy). This occurs in the learning of language, the gait of walking, the poise of sitting, preferences for foods, and the mode of driving a car or riding a bicycle. All require hours of practice, but once learned no longer require active attention. Many of the modern conditions of ill-health result from behaviours gradually adopted over time and are thus hard to challenge, including eating and drinking habits, smoking, sedentary lifestyles, reduced direct contacts with family and community, less active transport, reduced contact with green places, and increased use of pharmaceutical solutions to ill-health Will-power and focus are vital capabilities for learning skill-based habits. To learn a language (the first or more), arithmetic and times tables, to drive a vehicle, all require practice. The greater the cognitive control by the PFC, the less anxiety we suffer. In the Dunedin longitudinal study, children with the greatest willpower early in life had the best health outcomes during the life course. The critical years for children to learn self-control are 5–8 years of age: if they do, this improves cognitive capability Time outdoors as a child facilitates, and predicts, adult health

One enduring heuristic suggests it takes ten thousand hours to learn to become an expert Yet for most behaviours it is far fewer, as repetition sooner sends routines to the bottom brain. Repeated behaviours in consistent settings proceed more efficiently and are strengthened through association between situation (environmental cues) and action Experimental research has shown it takes 28 to 84 days to form a habit, depending on time spent per day, or ten weeks for healthy habits to become fixed Thirty minutes a day for 30 days of time in nature has been shown to improve well-being, mood, and mindfulness, though for this to become fixed as a habit, it is likely to need three times the number of days for long-term adherence Weekly interventions of walking and tai chi for 40 and 52 weeks have been shown to increase hippocampus volume in the elderly We thus suggest a rule of thumb of 50 days at one hour per day, or 100 days (approximately 3 months) at half an hour per day, to produce changes in the brain and result in fixes to behaviour. To improve or change a habituated routine, it needs to be brought back to the PFC, evaluated, and amended. But changing ingrained habits is hard: we must force the body to do something different as it will not choose voluntarily to do so. Habits must be brought back up to the blue brain and become subject to specific attention. In the increasingly typical modern life course, many people also give up activities that brought them pleasure on the grounds that they have neither the time nor the energy to continue. Over the life course, inch by inch, we cede territory to automated behaviours and habits that often bring discontent. We pay less attention to eating well, forget friends, and become less active. Halpern posed a question: when did you stop dancing? One significant policy and practice challenge is to identify the habit-releasers for improved health: new behaviours need forceful and sometimes fierce action. Other centres on the choice architecture of social and cultural environments that in turn shape choices about behaviours The U.K.'s Behavioural Insight Team, or Nudge Unit, has demonstrated how small nudges can lead to shifts in behaviours across large populations. But frequent practice is still required to fix new patterns in the brain: the fifty hours. The key concept is that the brain changes because of body behaviours: the property of neuroplasticity

6. Neuroplasticity and Placebos Neuroplasticity is the property of the brain to change structure and function by responding to actions by the body, to signals received from the external world, and to mental experiences. In this way, external and internal signals are not materially different: they are just signals. It is also understood that neurons that fire together, wire together; and those not used will die back. The conventional predominant view of the brain-mind is that if it breaks down, nothing can be done. The concept of neuroplasticity suggests new opportunities for directed or chosen changes across the life course. The first example centres on pain and pain control. Acute pain is a signal to attend to a problem immediately. But neuropathic–chronic pain is different: it comprises the incessant false alarms of the afterlife of acute pain. These repeated mental experiences cause structural changes in the brain, and the pain map continues expanding, and invading parts of the brain that process thought, sensations, images, and memory Persistent and chronic pain is also demoralising setting off new red alerts from the amygdala. An understanding of neuroplasticity has shown that the pain gate can be raised by endorphins, and these can be released by immersion-attentiveness activities such as mindfulness, meditation, and tai chi The gate rises, the pain sensations fall, and counter-stimulations in the invaded parts of the brain push away the pain memories. However, individuals must be relentless in forming this new habit: they must be more relentless than the pain that produced the map The placebo effect (PE) is a second example and is no less real because it is driven by thought. It causes as many changes in the brain as does medication. The placebo has long been conceptualised as an inert process, and thus used as an experimental control for drug testing. But recent research on the PE has shown the potential benefits of self-healing. The PE is a genuine phenomenon driven by expectancy in both patient and physicians/nurses, and has yielded beneficial clinical results for angina, bronchial asthma, herpes, ulcers, inflammatory bowel syndrome, and persistent pain The PE mechanism centres on the self-release of non-addictive endogenous opioids. It has been noted that alternative therapies with no clear scientific explanation but with elaborate rituals and beliefs can thus induce placebo effects, particularly if there is a good personal relationship between the practitioner and the patient It has also been shown that treatment augmented with warmth, attention, and confidence improves clinical outcomes. Patients thus engage in treating themselves if physicians, nurses, and carers have a friendly manner, engage in active listening, show empathy, allow periods of silence in conversation, and communicate confidence and positive expectations The British Medical Association has reinforced the importance of compassion and empathy for patient-centred care. In noting the high levels of

boredom on hospital wards, where there is too little physical activity, they have recommended hospitals engage in deliberate social activities, such as creative writing, music, visual art, dance, and singing. Better design would help too, including for creating healing gardens

7. Place Making

The green mind suggests that individuals link to natural places that are recognisable and individualised. These might include urban parks, gardens, nature reserves, and walking routes (including for dog walkers). In the contemporary affluent world, chronic place lessness has become endemic. People spend less time outdoors, travel less by walking and cycling, and move to a new house more often Children's disconnection from natural places stores up future problems, as fewer memories are made of life events in the critical middle age of childhood from 5 to 11 years The structure of physical and natural environments is now well-established as having an impact on physical and mental health with physical activity in cities by cycling and walking reducing cancer risk In an enriched environment, new neurons are produced by the hippocampus, which then turns short-term memories to long-term ones. Moderate activity, for example walking and tai chi, also produces new neurons in the hippocampus and increases hippocampus volume, thus improving memory Walking forwards into landscapes thus creates long-term memories; walking has also been shown to protect against the neurodegeneration that causes Parkinson's Disease (PD) and Huntington's Disease, delaying the onset of dementias by ten years. A sedentary, immobile lifestyle is less stimulating, causing parts of the brain to atrophy. A central problem in PD is inactivity, and medical treatment encourages passivity. Walking can help to cure it but may take a high degree of concentration to bring habits from the bottom brain to the top Exercise in natural places is as effective as fluoxetine (e.g., Prozac) for many people and tranquil scenes can quieten the mind

For better health and well-being, many people thus need behaviours that increase both memory- and place-making. Places are dense with meaning, stories, memories, and morals. They work on your mind the contours of our minds are shaped by places. Both gardening and allomothering promote recovery from stress and improve well-being; members of allotment groups experience less stress than same-age members of indoor groups Location can improve health, especially if the place is culturally considered as home Aboriginal groups returning to outstations have seen reductions in hypertension and diabetes Changes in well-being have been noted for Innu groups returning to the land in Labrador Aboriginal people describe land as a spiritual place, calm and centred, where the "quietness speaks to you" Natural and physically sensate environments appear to give more opportunities for immersive attention where there is a mix of mild continuing stimulation of the SNS and majority control by the calming PNS. Simms and Potts have argued for a new materialism in which is cultured a more pleasurable and respectful relationship with the world of things. Experiential purchases produce more enduring happiness than material purchase, with consumers deriving more benefits from anticipation, from the doing-experience, and from the memories created Finding fault with material consumption may appear to be seeking a return to living in a cave: it should not. The greater challenge is to increase individual well-being, reduce anxiety and depression, take more responsibility for the planet's future, and create an abundance of less

8. Linking Greener Minds to Contemplative and Greener Economies

Green Mind Theory offers an opportunity to link individual well-being to life behaviours and thus to whole economies. The future of the planet's natural capital relies on new patterns of material consumption that shift behaviours to sustainable consumption (activities that build natural capital rather than deplete it), and/or non-material consumption (activities with a light footprint on resources, but which deliver well-being, such as listening to bird song, gardening, talking, walking, and volunteering)

Green minds can build empathy and trust. They strengthen mirror neurons that show empathy, and oxytocin increases bonding between individuals and suppresses the red alert nature of the amygdala Some traditions call this increasing the circle of us, acknowledging the secret history of our enemies: they too feel sorrow and suffering, and ten thousand things may have caused them to act. A green and prosocial mind puts an emphasis on giving, contributing, and volunteering. Volunteers have higher well-being than non-volunteers, greater life satisfaction across the life course, and live two years longer than non-volunteers Empathy would have been highly selected within group and bands during hominid evolution, and we search for it today. In hospital settings, patients are already on red alert: they are anxious and worried. In the U.S., those surgeons sued the most do not make more mistakes, they were just unable to establish trust and empathy with patients Nurses and doctors who spend more time with patients smile and treat them as individuals and are themselves happier; those patients also recover more rapidly and need less pain control. Porsche is a component of many contemplative traditions: acute attention to and immersion in the present moment Porsche moves in two directions: inwards into the mind, and outwards to the natural world and other people. More equal societies do better for all; inequality is bad for all Optimists live 19% longer than pessimists, suggesting that expectations about the future affect current well-being A popular assumption for the past half century has been that increased material consumption and rising GDP inevitably increases well-being. There have been many technological improvements to lives, yet timeless consumer culture invents new pleasures, often producing more suffering from second arrows: either we cannot access apparent pleasures, or when we do have them, they deliver less than expected, rapidly losing their lustre. One priority is to redefine prosperity, and by substituting activities that improve social cohesion, mental and physical well-being, and memory creation, the impact on natural capital and ecosystem services could be reduced whilst improving well-being

Green growth and the green economy have become important targets for national and international organisations, including the OECD, UNEP, the World Bank, the Rio+20 conference, and the Global Green Growth Initiative UNEP defines the green economy as "resulting in human well-being and social equity, while significantly reducing environmental risks and ecological scarcities". To date, many countries acknowledge the need for greener economies, but few have acted significantly. Notable exceptions include: China's launch of eco-civilisation policies, Korea's building an advanced carbon economy, Kenya's use of feed-in-tariffs dramatically to increase renewable sources of energy, and Denmark's production of more energy from wind than it consumes nationally.

Greener economies will not look much like the current economy. They will be disruptive but less than the impact of severe climate change. The notion of a greener and prosocial economy further implies a cultural understanding of how much is enough A key challenge is how a mode of consumption based on enough not more can be created, so resulting in mass behaviours of enounces Wood et al. have demonstrated the value of gratitude to well-being, and how it arises both from the receipt of aid/support from others and from an internal appreciation of the positive aspects of life. They conclude that people would be better off spending time amassing friendships and appreciating what they have rather than seeking higher incomes and amassing material possessions. In greener economies, different forms of contemplative consumption will be valued, such as of storytelling, engaging with nature, and skill-based crafts. They tend to be cooperative, enhancing social capital formation and reducing inequity. This will bring positive feedbacks, as prosocial behaviours cause others to be prosocial, thus building social capital They offer four options to consumers: resist consumerism by opting out (e.g., downshifting, voluntary simplicity), retain possessions for longer (before replacement), make different choices (ethical or green consumerism), and substitute non-material consumption activities (e.g., nature consumption) [5]. Part of the solution for greener economies is the adoption of activities that lead to green minds. The Caerphilly Cohort Study has, though, shown that there was no change in the adoption of healthy behaviours by men over 30 years (commencing 1979): those with four of five behaviours (non-smoking, acceptable body mass, high fruit and vegetable consumption, regular activity, and low-moderate alcohol intake) delayed onset of heart disease by 12 years alongside reduced cognitive impairment and a delayed onset of dementia But those starting with low adoption did not change over time, even though public knowledge of these risks has grown. Kvaavik et al. showed in a population of 5000 adults that the adoption of healthy behaviours extended life by a mean of 12 years.

9. Priorities for Implementing Healthy Habits

What does the Green Mind concept suggest for instruction and implementation? We have observed that the future of the planet relies on substitution of non-material consumption, making more of activities with a light footprint, and the co-delivery of well-being. But the history of implementation of healthy habits in affluent countries is not encouraging. There are five levels for possible action: International agreements: these are rare, slow to implement, and easy to free-ride or undermine. National policies: few successes for whole populations, so far, though anti-smoking and seat-belt legislation are successes. Institutional and sectoral policies and practice: the potential for government, employers, and charitable organisations to change practices to affect large numbers of people, such as in education, mental health, social care, or hospitals.

Community actions and ceremonies: already widespread and manifested in local groups and rituals but undervalued and not yet widely used to improve well-being.

Voluntary actions of individuals: hard to sustain, though the most pushed by governments.

Elements 1 and 2 are hard to achieve, and 5 is often too easy to demand: it will be institutions and communities that are likely to reach the largest number of people quickly. We propose an emphasis on nature, social, and craft engagements in neighbourhoods, schools, care homes, and health care facilities (Table 3). Environmental organisations and charities have a vital role to play promoting healthy engagement with nature as part of their missions. Employers also can act by focusing on work-life balance, and activities that contribute to well-being. Core intervention priorities should thus centre on hard-to-reach populations and cohorts, and those for whom current policies and treatment are struggling to find solutions. This includes those in certain age groups, such as children and the elderly, and those suffering from lifestyle-related conditions, such as obesity, type 2 diabetes, loneliness, and mental ill-health. These interventions are variously called Nature-Based Interventions (NBIs), Wise Psychological

Interventions (WPIs), and Positive Psychological Interventions and offer opportunities for individual as well as collective restoration

Table 3. Nature, social, and craft engagements that build the green mind.

Table

The risk of death is reduced and longevity increased through social group membership and social support through interesting and healthy diets through cognitive engagement with craft and mindfulness/spiritual activities through physically-active lifestyles, such as in the Sardinian mountains Okinawa Harvard alumni and Caerphilly men Combinations of all can lead to exceptional longevity It thus appears that extreme longevity is promoted by the habitual consumption of healthy food, daily physical activity, an engagement with nature, strong social capital, and cognitive engagement. These also offer the prospect of living well and with contentment.

We propose twelve research questions to focus action on children, adults, healthy longevity, and redesign.

9.1. Children

Young children are becoming increasingly socially-disconnected, inactive, and eating badly: what green mind interventions would work best for 5–11-year olds?

How protective would such interventions be across the life course?

9.2. Adults

How can immersive-attention activities be promoted to produce health and well-being improvements across whole populations (including the dissipation of unhealthy habits)?

What are the best policies for local and national governments to implement that would aid such adoption and desorption?

What priority activities and behaviours should be promoted at stressful transition points in the life course (moving schools, transition to university, becoming a parent, marriage and divorce, deaths of friends and relatives, retirement, transition to social care)?

9.3. Longevity

What green mind interventions offer the greatest efficacy for health outcomes in elderly populations and social care settings?

How can interventions based on outdoor activity, social interactions, good food, and cognitive engagement be best implemented?

What can be learned from cultures where healthy living continues into the 8th–11th decades of the life course (such as in the longevity hotspots of Nagano and Okinawa in Japan)?

9.4. Redesign

What well-being and health outcomes could be delivered in hospitals and care settings if green and prosocial design was implemented?

How much real income could be saved by hospitals from promoting behaviours that prevented the need for treatment?

How can human settlements be redesigned to increase engagement with existing green spaces?

Could some solutions to climate change rest in the green mind and its capacity to drive low consumption behaviours?

We conclude by setting out a ten-point call to action based on compelling supportive scientific evidence about the influence of lifestyle and behaviour on short- and long-term well-being (Table 4). None of this will be easy to achieve at the population level. It will require behaviour change and habit formation; it will require changes in infrastructure, policies, and resourcing. But every small contemplative undertaking can lead to the gradual formation of a green mind. It just needs relentless persistence long enough to form the habit. As indicated above, it will be institutions and communities that are likely to reach the largest number of people quickly. There could be emphasis on nature, social, and craft engagements in neighbourhoods, schools, care homes, and health care facilities. Environmental organisations and charities could play a vital role in promoting healthy engagement with nature as part of their missions. Every child could be outdoors every day; every older person in a care home could sit in a garden. Every economy could be green and prosocial. Now is time for a new ethic: the economy is the environment. Nature will survive us all.

Table 4. Ten calls to action for the green mind.

Table

Conclusions

Comments on the Green Mind

Nudge tactics and policy changes have now made it possible in some countries to imagine the reality of an entirely tobacco-free culture, or where some water and air systems are pollution-free. In others, hunger has been dramatically reduced. What level, thus, of ambition is possible when considering policies and practices that could mostly solve lifestyle-related conditions and diseases typical of modern, high material-consumption cultures, utilizing the Green Mind Theory? Is it possible to imagine substantial reductions in incidence of mental ill-health, obesity, type 2 diabetes, loneliness, physical inactivity, and cardiovascular disease through the adoption of resilient green mind habits, fostering prosocial and greener economies across whole populations? We suggest Green Mind Theory offers some new opportunities to address these pervasive challenges by suggesting new routes to raising the well-being baseline of whole populations though the adoption of healthier habits and behaviours.

Theory of Mind

Theory of Mind is the branch of cognitive science that investigates how we ascribe mental states to other persons and how we use the states to explain and predict the actions of those other persons. More accurately, it is the branch that investigates mindreading or mentalizing or mentalistic abilities. These skills are shared by almost all human beings beyond early childhood. They are used to treat other agents as the bearers of unobservable psychological states and processes, and to anticipate and explain the agents' behaviour in terms of such states and processes. These mentalistic abilities are also called "folk psychology" by philosophers, and "naïve psychology" and "intuitive psychology" by cognitive scientists. It is important to note that Theory of Mind is not an appropriate term to characterize this research area (and neither to denote our mentalistic abilities) since it seems to assume right from the start the validity of a specific account of the nature and development of mindreading, that is, the view that it depends on the deployment of a theory of the mental realm, analogous to the theories of the physical world ("naïve physics"). But this view—known as theory-theory—is only one of the accounts offered to explain our mentalistic abilities. In contrast, theorists of mental simulation have suggested that what lies at the root of mindreading is not any sort of folk-psychological conceptual scheme, but rather a kind of mental modelling in which the simulator uses her own mind as an analogy model of the mind of the simulated agent. Both theory-theory and simulation-theory are families of theories. Some theory-theorists maintain that our naïve theory of mind is the product of the scientific-like exercise of a domain-general theorizing capacity. Other theory-theorists defend a quite different hypothesis, according to which mindreading rests on the maturation of a mental organ dedicated to the domain of psychology. Simulation-theory also shows different facets. According to the "moderate" version of simulations, mental concepts are not completely excluded from simulation. Simulation be a process through which we first generate, and self-attribute pretend mental states that are intended to correspond to those of the simulated agent, and then project them onto the target. By contrast, the "radical" version of simulations rejects the primacy of first-person mindreading and contends that we imaginatively transform ourselves into the simulated agent, interpreting the target's behaviour without using any kind of mental concept, not even ones referring to ourselves. Finally, the claim common to both theorists of theory and theorists of simulation that mindreading plays a primary role in human social understanding was challenged in the early 21st century, mainly by phenomenology-oriented philosophers and cognitive scientists.

Table of Contents

Theory-

The Child-Scientist Theory

The Modularise Theory-

First-Person Mindreading and Theory-

Simulation-Theory

Simulation with and without Introspection

Simulation in Low-Level Mindreading

Social Cognition without Mindreading

References and Further Reading

1. Theory-

Social psychologists have investigated mindreading since at least the 1940s. In Heider and Simmel's (1944) classic studies, participants were presented with animated events involving interacting geometric shapes. When asked to report what they saw, the participants almost invariably treated these shapes as intentional agents with motives and purposes, suggesting the existence of an automatic capacity for mentalistic attribution. Pursuing this line of research would lead to Heider's The Psychology of Interpersonal Relations (1958), a seminal book which is one of the main historical referents of the scientific inquiry into our mentalistic practice. In this book Heider characterizes "common sense psychology" as a sophisticated conceptual scheme that has an influence on human perception and action in the social world comparable to that which Kant's categorical framework has on human perception and action in the physical world (see Male & Ickes 2000: 201).

Heider's visionary work played a central role in the origination and definition of attribution theory, that is, the field of social psychology that investigates the mechanisms underlying ordinary explanations of our own and other people's behaviour. However, attribution theory is a quite different way of approaching our mentalistic practice. Heider took common sense psychology in its real value of knowledge, arguing that scientific psychology has a good deal to learn from it. In contrast, most research on causal attribution has been faithful to behaviourism's methodological lesson and focused on the epistemic inaccuracy of common-sense psychology. Two years before Heider's book, Wilfred Sellars' (1956) Empiricism and the Philosophy of Mind had suggested that our grasp of mental phenomena does not originate from direct access to our inner life, but is the result of a "folk" theory of mind, which we acquire through some form or other of enculturation. Sellars' speculation turned out to be very philosophically productive and in agreement with social-psychology research on self-attribution, coming to be known as "Theory-Theory" (a term coined by Morton 1980—henceforth "TT"). During the 1970s one or other form of TT was a very effective antidote to Cartesians and philosophical behaviourism. In particular, TT was coupled with Nagel's (1961) classic account of intertheoretical reduction as deduction of the reduced from the reducing theory via bridge principles in order to turn the ontological problem of the relationship between the mental and the physical into a more tractable epistemological problem concerning the relations between theories. Thus it became possible to take a notion—intertheoretical reduction—rigorously studied by philosophers of science; to examine the relations between folk psychology as a theory including the common sense mentalistic ontology and its scientific successors (scientific psychology, neuroscience, or some other form of science of the mental); and to let ontological/metaphysical questions be answered by (I) focusing on questions about explanation and theory reduction first and foremost, and then (ii) depending on how those first questions were answered, drawing the appropriate ontological/metaphysical conclusions based on a comparison with how similar questions about explanation and reduction got answered in other scientific episodes and the ontological conclusions philosophers and scientists drew in those cases (this strategy is labelled "the intertheoretical-reduction reformulation of the mind-body problem" in Buckle 2003). In this context, TT was taken as the major premise in the standard argument for eliminative materialism (see Ramsey 2011: §2.1). In its strongest form, eliminative predicts that part or all of our folk-psychological theory will vanish into thin air, just as it happened in the past when scientific progress led to the abandonment of the folk theory of witchcraft or the prescientific theories of phlogiston and caloric fluid. This prediction rests on an argument which moves from considering folk psychology as a massively defective theory to the conclusion that—just as with witches, phlogiston, and caloric fluid—folk-psychological entities do not exist. Thus philosophy of mind joined attribution theory in adopting a critical attitude toward the explanatory adequacy of folk psychology (see, for example, Stich's 1983 eliminability doubts about the folk concept of belief, motivated inter alia by the experimental social psychology literature on dissonance and self-attribution). Notice, however, that TT can be differently construed depending on whether we adopt a personal or sub personal perspective (see Stich & Ravenscroft 1994: §4). The debate between intentional realists and eliminative favoured David Lewis' personal-level formulation of TT. According to Lewis, the folk theory of mind is implicit in our everyday talk about mental states. We entertain "platitudes" regarding the causal relations of mental states, sensory stimuli, and motor responses that can be systematized (or "Ramified"). The result is a functionalist theory that gives the terms of mentalistic vocabulary their meaning in the same way as scientific theories define their theoretical terms, namely "as the occupants of the causal roles specified by the theory…; as the entities, whatever those may be, that bear certain causal relations to one another and to the referents of the O[observational]-terms" (Lewis 1972: 211). In this perspective, mindreading can be described as an exercise in reflective reasoning, which involves the application of general reasoning abilities to premises including ceteris paribus folk-psychological generalizations. A good example of this conception of mindreading is Grice's schema for the derivation of conversational implicatures: He said that P; he could not have done this unless he thought that Q; he knows (and knows that I know that he knows) that I will realize that it is necessary to suppose that Q; he has done nothing to stop me thinking that Q; so he intends me to think, or is at least willing for me to think, that Q(Grice 1989: 30-1; cit. in Wilson 2005: 1133). Since the end of the 1970s, however, primatology, developmental psychology, cognitive neuropsychiatry, and empirically informed philosophy have been contributing to a collaborative inquiry into TT. In the context of this literature the term "theory" refers to a "tacit" or "sub-doxastic" structure of knowledge, a corpus of internally represented information that guides the execution of mentalistic capacities. But then the functionalist theory that fixes the meaning of mentalistic terms is not the theory implicit in our everyday, mentalistic talk, but the tacit theory (in Chomsky's sense) sub serving our thought and talk about the mental realm (see Stich & Nichols 2003: 241). On this perspective, the inferential processes that depend on the theory have an automatic and unconscious character that distinguishes them from reflective reasoning processes. In developmental psychology part of the basis for the study of mindreading skills in children was already in Jean Piaget's seminal work on egocentrism in the 1930s to 50s, and the work on metacognition (especially metamemory) in the 1970s. But the developmental research on mindreading took off only under the thrust of three discoveries in the 1980s (see Leslie 1998). First, normally developing 2-year-olds can engage in pretend play. Second, normally developing children undergo a deep change in their understanding of the psychological states of other people somewhere between the ages of 3 and 4, as indicated especially by the appearance of their ability to solve a variety of "false-belief" problems (see immediately below). Lastly, children diagnosed with autism spectrum disorders are especially impaired in attributing mental states to other people. Swimmer & Penner (1983) provided the theory-of-mind research with a seminal experimental paradigm: the "false-belief task." In the most well-known version of this task, a child watches two puppets interacting in a room. One puppet ("Sally") puts a toy in location A and then leaves the room. While Sally is out of the room, the other puppet ("Anne") moves the toy from location A to location B. Sally returns to the room, and the child onlooker is asked where she will look for her toy, in location A or in location B. Now, 4- and 5-year-olds have little difficulty passing this test, judging that Sally will look for her toy in location A although it really is in location B. These correct answers provide evidence that the child realizes that Sally does not know that the toy has been moved, and so will act upon a false belief. Many younger children, typically 3-year-olds, fail such a task, often asserting that Sally will look for the toy in the place where it was moved. Dozens of versions of this task have now been used, and while the precise age of success varies between children and between task versions, in general we can confidently say that children begin to successfully perform the ("verbal") false-belief tasks at around 4 years (see the meta-analysis in Wellman et al. 2001; see also below, the reference to "non-verbal" false-belief tasks).

Swimmer and Penner's false-belief task set off a flood of experiments concerning the infant understanding of the mind. In this context, the first hypotheses about the process of acquisition of the naïve theory of mind were suggested. The finding that mentalistic skills emerge very early, in the first 3-4 years, and in a way relatively independent from the development of other cognitive abilities, led some scholars (for example, Simon Baron-Cohen, Jerry Feodor, Alan Leslie) to conceive them as the end-state of the endogenous maturation of an innate theory-of-mind module (or system of modules). This contrasted with the view of other researchers (for example, Alison Gopnik, Josef Penner, Henry Wellman), who maintained that the intuitive theory of mind develops in childhood in a manner comparable to the development of scientific theories.

a. The Child-Scientist Theory

According to a first version of TT, "the child (as little) scientist theory," the body of internally-represented knowledge that drives the exercise of mentalistic abilities has much the same structure as a scientific theory, and it is acquired, stored, and used in much the same way that scientific theories are: by formulating explanations, making predictions, and then revising the theory or modifying auxiliary hypotheses when the predictions fail. Gopnik & Meltzoff (1997) put forward this idea in its more radical form. They argue that the body of knowledge underlying mindreading has all the structural, functional, and dynamic features that, on their view, characterize most scientific theories. One of the most important features is defeasibility. As it happens in scientific practice, the child's naïve theory of mind can also be "annulled," that is, replaced when an accumulation of counterevidence to it occurs. The child-scientist theory is, therefore, akin to Piaget's constructivism insofar as it depicts the cognitive development in childhood and early adolescence as a succession of increasingly sophisticated naïve theories. For instance, Wellman (1990) has argued that around age 4 children become able to pass the false-belief tests because they move from an elementary "copy" theory of mind to a fully "representational" theory of mind, which allows them to acknowledge the explanatory role of false beliefs. The child-scientist theory inherits from Piaget not only the constructivist framework but also the idea that the cognitive development is a process that depends on a domain-general learning mechanism. A domain-general (or general-purpose) psychological structure is one that can be used to do problem solving across many different content domains; it contrasts with a domain-specific psychological structure, which is dedicated to solving a restricted class of problems in a restricted content domain (see Samuels 2000). Now, Piaget's model of cognitive development posits an innate endowment of reflexes and domain-general learning mechanisms, which enable the child to set up sensorimotor interactions with the environment that unfold a steady improvement in the capacity of problem-solving in any cognitive domain—physical, biological, psychological, and so forth. Analogously, Gopnik & Schulz (2004, 2007) have argued that the learning mechanism that supports all cognitive development is a domain-general Bayesian mechanism that allows children to extract causal structure from patterns of data. Another theory-theorist who endorses a domain-general conception of cognitive development is Josef Penner (1991). On his view, it is the appearance of the ability to meet represent that enables the 4-year-olds to shift from a "situation theory" to a "representation theory," and thus pass false-belief tests. Children are situation theorists by the age of around 2 years. At 3 they possess a concept, "prolife" (or "bedance"), in which the concepts of pretend and belief coexist undifferentiated. The concept of prolife allows the child to understand that a person can "act as if" something was such and such (for example, as if "this banana is a telephone") when it is not. At 4 children acquire a representational concept of belief which enables them to understand that, like the public representations, inner representations can also misrepresent states of affairs (see Penner, Baker & Hutton 1994). Thus, Penner suggests that children first learn to understand the properties of public (pictorial and linguistic) representations; only in a second moment they extend, through a process of analogical reasoning, these characteristics to mental representations. On this perspective, then, the concept of belief is the product of a domain-general metarepresentational capacity that includes but is not limited to metarepresentational of mental states. (But for criticism, see Harris 2000, who argues that pretence and belief are very different and are readily distinguished by context by 3-year olds.)

b. The Modularise Theory-

According to the child-scientist theory, children learn the naïve theory of mind in much the same way that adults learn about scientific theories. By contrast, the modularise version of TT holds that the body of knowledge underlying mindreading lacks the structure of a scientific theory, being stored in one or more innate modules, which gradually become functional ("mature") during infant development. Inside the module the body of information can be stored as a suite of domain-specific computational mechanisms; or as a system of domain-specific representations; or in both ways (see Simpson et al. 2005: 13).

The notion of modularity as domain-specificity, whose paradigm is Noam Chomsky's module of language, informs the so-called "core knowledge" hypothesis, according to which human cognition builds on a repertoire of domain-specific systems of knowledge. Studies of children and adults in diverse cultures, human infants, and non-human primates provide evidence for at least four systems of knowledge that serve to represent significant aspects of the environment: inanimate objects and their motions; agents and their goal-directed actions; places and their geometric relations; sets and their approximate numerical relation. These are systems of domain-specific, task-specific representations, which are shared by other animals, persist in adults, and show little variation by culture, language, or sex (see Carey & Selke 1996; Selke & Kindler 2007).

And yet a domain-specific body of knowledge is an "inert" psychological structure, which gives rise to behaviour only if it is manipulated by some cognitive mechanism. The question arises, then, whether the domain-specific body of information that sub serves mentalistic abilities is the database of either a domain-specific or domain-general computational system. In some domains, a domain-specific computational mechanism and a domain-specific body of information can form a single mechanism (for example, a parser is very likely to be a domain-specific computational mechanism that manipulates a domain-specific data structure). But in other domains, as Samuels (1998, 2000) has noticed, domain-specific systems of knowledge might be computed by domain-general rather than domain-specific algorithms (but for criticism, see Carruthers 2006 The existence of a domain-specific algorithm that exploits a body of information specific to the domain of naïve psychology has been proposed by Alan Leslie (1994, 2000). He postulated a specialized component of social intelligence, the "Theory-of-Mind Mechanism" (Tommy), which receives as input information about the past and present behaviour of other people and utilizes this information to compute their probable psychological states. The outputs of Tommy are descriptions of psychological states in the form of met representations or M-representations, that is, agent-cantered descriptions of behaviour, which include a triadic relation that specifies four kinds of information: (I) an agent, (ii) an informational relation that specifies the agent's attitude (pretending, believing, desiring, and so forth), (iii) an aspect of reality that grounds the agent's attitude, (iv) the content of the agent's attitude. Therefore, to pretend and understand others' pretending, the child's Tommy is supposed to output the M-representation <Mother PRETENDS (of) this banana (that) "it is a telephone">. Analogously, to predict Sally's behaviour in the false-belief test, Tommy is supposed to output the M-representation <Sally BELIEVES (of) her marble (that) "it is in the basket">. (Note that Leslie coined the term "M-representation" to distinguish his own concept of meta-representation from Penner's 1991. For Penner uses the term at a personal level to refer to the child's conscious theory of representation, whereas Leslie utilizes the term at a sub personal level to designate an unconscious data structure computed by an information-processing mechanism. See Leslie & Thais 1992: 231, note 2.) In the 1980s, Leslie's Tommy hypothesis was the basis for the development of a neuropsychological perspective on autism.

Children suffering from this neurodevelopmental disorder exhibit a triad of impairments: social incompetence, poor verbal and nonverbal communicative skills, and a lack of pretend play. Because social competence, communication, and pretending all rest on mentalistic abilities, Baron-Cohen, Frith & Leslie (1985) speculated that the autistic triad might be the result of an impaired Tommy. This hypothesis was investigated in an experiment in which typically developing 4-year-olds, children with autism (12 years; IQ 82), and children with Down syndrome (10 years; IQ 64) were tested on the Sally and Ann false-belief task. Eighty-five percent of the normally developing children and 86% of the children with Down syndrome passed the test; but only 20% of the autistic children predicted that Sally would look in the basket. This is one of the first examples of psychiatry driven by cognitive neuropsychology (followed by Christopher Frith's 1992 theory of schizophrenia as late-onset autism). According to Leslie, the Tommy is the specific innate basis of basic mentalistic abilities, which matures during the infant's second year. In support of this hypothesis, he cites inter alia his analysis of pretend play that would show that 18-month-old children are able to meet represent the propositional attitude of pretending. This analysis results, however, in an immediate empirical problem. If the Tommy is fully functional at 18 months, why are children unable to successfully perform false-belief tasks until they are around 4 years old? Leslie's hypothesis is that although the concept of belief is already in place in children younger than 4, in the false-belief tasks this concept is masked by immaturity in another capacity that is necessary for good performance on the task—namely inhibitory control. Since, by default, the Tommy attributes a belief with content that reflects current reality, to succeed in a false-belief task this default attribution must be inhibited and an alternative nonfactual content for the belief selected instead. This is the task of an executive control mechanism that Leslie calls "Selection Processor" (SP). Thus 3-year-olds fail standard false-belief tasks because they possess the Tommy but not yet the inhibitory SP (see Leslie & Thais 1992; Leslie & Palazzi 1998). The Tommy/SP model seems to find support in a series of experiments that test understanding of false mental and public representations in normal and autistic children. Leslie & Thais (1992) have found that normal 3-year-olds fail the standard false-belief tasks, the two non-mental meta-representational tests, the false-map task and Zaitchik's (1990) outdated-photograph task. In contrast, autistic children are at or near ceiling on the non-mental metarepresentational tests but fail false-belief tasks. Normal 4-year-olds can succeed in all these tasks. According to Leslie and Thais, the Tommy/SP model can account for these findings: normal 3-year-olds possess the Tommy but not yet SP; autistic children are impaired in Tommy but not in SP; normal 4-year-olds possess both the Tommy and an adequate SP. By contrast, these results appear to be counterevidence to Penner's idea that children first understand public representations before then applying that understanding to mental states. If this were right, then autistic children should have difficulty with both kinds of representations. And in fact Penner (1993) suggests that the autistic deficit is due to a genetic impairment of the mechanisms that sub serve attention shifting, a damage that interferes with the formation of the database required for the development of a theory of representation in general. But what autistics' performance in mental and non-mental metarepresentational tasks seems to show is a dissociation between understanding false maps and outdated photographs, on one hand, and understanding false beliefs, on the other. A finding that can be easily explained in the context of Leslie's domain-specific approach to mindreading, according to which children with autism have a specific deficit in understanding mental representation but not representation in general. In support of this interpretation, fMRI studies showed that activity in the right temporo-parietal junction is high while participants are thinking about false beliefs, but no different from resting levels while participants are thinking about outdated photographs or false maps or signs. This suggests a neural substrate for the behavioural dissociation between pictorial and mental metarepresentational abilities (see Saxe & Kanwisher 2003; for a critical discussion of the domain-specificity interpretation of these behavioural and neuroimaging data, see Germans & Stone 2008; Penner & Eichhorn 2008; Penner & Leek am 2008). Leslie (2005) recruits new data to support his claim that mental metarepresentational abilities emerge from a specialized neurocognitive mechanism that matures during the second year of life. Standard false-belief tasks are "elicited-response" tasks in which children are asked a direct question about an agent's false belief. But investigations using "spontaneous-response" tasks (Oishi & Baillargeon 2005) seem to suggest that the ability to attribute false beliefs is present much earlier, at the age of 15 months (even at 13 months in Saurian, Cali & Sperber 2007). However, Leslie's mentalistic interpretation of these data has been challenged by Ruffman & Penner (2005), who have proposed an explanation of Oishi and Baillargeon's results that assumes that the infants might be employing a non-mentalistic behaviour-rule such as, "People look for objects where last seen" (for replies, see Baillargeon et al. 2010). The Tommy has been considered, contra Feodor, as one of the strongest candidates for central modularity (see, for example, Cotterill & Carruthers 1999: 67-8). However, Samuels (2006: 47) has objected that it is difficult to establish whether the Tommy's domain of application is central cognition. He suggests that the question is still more controversial in light of Leslie's proposal of modelling Tommy as a relatively low-level mechanism of selective attention, whose functioning depends on SP, which is a non-modular mechanism, penetrable to knowledge and instruction (see Leslie, Friedman & German 2004).

c. First-Person Mindreading and Theory-During the 1980s and 1990s most of the work in Theory of Mind was concerned with the mechanisms that sub serve the attribution of psychological states to others (third-person mindreading). In the last decade, however, an increasing number of psychologists and philosophers have also proposed accounts of the mechanisms underlying the attribution of psychological states to oneself (first-person mindreading). For most theory-theorists, first-person mindreading is an interpretative activity that depends on mechanisms that capitalize on the same theory of mind used to attribute mental states to other agents. Such mechanisms are triggered by information about mind-external states of affairs, essentially the target's behaviour and/or the situation in which it occurs/occurred. The claim is, then, that there is a functional symmetry between first-person and third-person mentalistic attribution—the "outside access" view of introspection in Robbins the "symmetrical" or "self/other parity" account of self-knowledge in Schnitzel (2010).

The first example of a symmetrical account of self-knowledge is Beam's (1972) "self-perception theory." With reference to Skinner's methodological guidance, but with a position that reveals affinities with symbolic interactionism, Bam holds that one knows one's own inner states (for example, attitudes and emotions) through a process completely analogous to that occurring when one knows other people' inner states, that is, by inferring them from the observation/recollection of one's own behaviour and/or the circumstances in which it occurs/occurred. The TT version of the symmetrical account of self-knowledge develops Beam's approach by claiming that observations and recollections of one's own behaviour and the circumstances in which it occurs/occurred are the input of mechanisms that exploit theories that apply to the same extent to ourselves and to others. In the well-known social-psychology experiments reviewed by Nisbett & Wilson (1977), the participants' attitudes and behaviour were caused by motivational factors inaccessible to consciousness—such factors as cognitive dissonance, numbers of bystanders in a public crisis, positional and "halo" effects and subliminal cues in problem solving and semantic disambiguation, and so on. However, when explicitly asked about the motivations (causes) of their actions, the subjects did not hesitate to state, sometimes with great eloquence, their very reasonable motives. Nisbett and Wilson explained this pattern of results by arguing that the subjects did not have any direct access to the real causes of their attitudes and behaviour; rather, they engaged in an activity of confabulation, that is, they exploited a priori causal theories to develop reasonable but imaginary explanations of the motivational factors of their attitudes and behaviour (see also Johansson et al. 2006, where Nisbett and Wilson's legacy is developed through a new experimental paradigm to study introspection, the "choice blindness" paradigm). Evidence for the symmetrical account of self-knowledge comes from Nisbett & Bellows' (1977) utilization of the so-called "actor-observer paradigm." In one experiment they compared the introspective reports of participants ("actors") to the reports of a control group of "observers" who were given a general description of the situation and asked to predict how the actors would react. Observers' predictions were found to be statistically identical to—and as inaccurate as—the reports by the actors. This finding suggests that "both groups produced these reports via the same route, namely by applying or generating similar causal theories" (Nisbett & Wilson 1977: 250-1; see also Schnitzel 2010: §§2.1.2 and 4.2.1).

In developmental psychology Alison Gopnik (1993) has defended a symmetrical account of self-knowledge by arguing that there is good developmental evidence of developmental synchronies: children's understanding of themselves proceeds in lockstep with their understanding of others. For example, since TT assumes that first-person and third-person mentalistic attributions are both sub served by the same theory of mind, it predicts that if the theory is not yet equipped to solve certain third-person false-belief problems, then the child should also be unable to perform the parallel first-person task. A much-discussed instance of parallel performance on tasks for self and other is in Gopnik & Astington (1988). In the "Smarties Box" experiment, children were shown with the candy container for the British confection "Smarties" and were asked what they thought was in the container. Naturally they answered "Smarties." The container was then opened to reveal not Smarties, but a pencil. Children were then asked a series of questions, including "What will [your friend] say is in the box?", and successively "When you first saw the box, before we opened it, what did you think was inside it?". It turned out that the children's ability to answer the question concerning oneself was significantly correlated with their ability to answer the question concerning another. (See also the above-cited Wellman et al. 2001, which offers meta-analytic findings to the effect that performance on false-belief tasks for self and for others is virtually identical at all ages.) Data from autism have also been used to motivate the claim that first-person and third person mentalistic attribution has a common basis. An intensely debated piece of evidence comes from a study by Hurlburt, Happen & Frith (1994), in which three people suffering from Asperger syndrome were tested with the descriptive experience sampling method. In this experimental paradigm, subjects are instructed to carry a random beeper, pay attention to the experience that was ongoing at the moment of the beep, and jot down notes about that now-immediately-past experience (see Hurlburt & Schnitzel 2007). The study showed marked qualitative differences in introspection in the autistic subjects: unlike normal subjects who report several different phenomenal state types—including inner verbalisation, visual images, unsymbolised thinking, and emotional feelings—the first two autistic subjects reported visual images only; the third subject could report no inner experience at all. According to Frith & Happen (1999: 14), this evidence strengthens the hypothesis that self-awareness, like other awareness, is dependent on the same theory of mind. Thus, evidence from social psychology, development psychology and cognitive neuropsychiatry makes a case for a symmetrical account of self-knowledge. As Schnitzel (2010: §2.1.3) rightly notes, however, no one advocates a thoroughly symmetrical conception because some margin is always left for some sort of direct self-knowledge. Nisbett & Wilson (1977: 255), for example, draw a sharp distinction between "cognitive processes" (the causal processes underlying judgments, decisions, emotions, sensations) and mental "content" (those judgments, decisions, emotions, sensations themselves). Subjects have "direct access" to this mental content, and this allows them to know it "with near certainty." In contrast, they have no access to the processes that cause behaviour. However, insofar as Nisbett and Wilson do not propose any hypothesis about this alleged direct self-knowledge, their theory is incomplete.

In order to offer an account of this supposedly direct self-knowledge, some philosophers made a more or less radical return to various forms of Cartesians, construing first-person mindreading as a process that permits the access to at least some mental phenomena in a relatively direct and non-interpretative way. On this perspective, introspective access does not appeal to theories that serve to interpret "external" information, but rather exploits mechanisms that can receive information about inner life through a relatively direct channel—the "inside access" view of introspection in Robbins (2006: 618); the "self-detection" account of self-knowledge in Schnitzel (2010: §2.2). The inside access view comes in various forms. Mentalistic self-attribution may be realized by a mechanism that processes information about the functional profile of mental states, or their representational content, or both kinds of information (see Robbins 2006: 618; for a "neural" version of the inside access view, see below, §2a). A representationalism-functionalist version of the inside access view is Nichols & Stich's (2003) account of first-person mindreading in terms of "monitoring mechanisms." The authors begin by drawing a distinction between detection and inference. It is one thing to detect mental states, it is another to reason about mental states, that is, using information about mental states to predict and explain one's own or other people's mental states and behaviour. Moreover, both the attribution of a mental state and the inferences that one can make about it can be referred to oneself or other people. Thus, we get four possible operations: first- and third-person detection, first- and third-person reasoning. Now, Nichols and Stich's hypothesis is that whereas third-person detecting and first- and third-person reasoning are all sub served by the same theory of mind, the mechanism for detecting one's own mental states is quite independent of the mechanism that deals with the mental states of other people. More precisely, the Monitoring Mechanism (MM) theory assumes the existence of a suite of distinct self-monitoring computational mechanisms, including one for monitoring and providing self-knowledge of one's own experiential states, and one for monitoring and providing self-knowledge of one's own propositional attitudes. Thus, for example, if X believes that p, and the proper MM is activated, it copies the representation p in X's "Belief Box", embeds the copy in a representation schema of the form "I believe that and then places this second-order representation back in X's Belief Box. Since the MM theory assumes that first-person mindreading does not involve mechanisms of the sort that figure in third-person mindreading, it implies that the first capacity should be dissociable, both diachronically and synchronically, from the second. In support of this prediction Nichols & Stich (2003) cite developmental data to the effect that, on a wide range of tasks, instead of the parallel performance predicted by TT, children exhibit developmental asynchronies. For example, children are capable of attributing knowledge and ignorance to themselves before they can attribute those states to others (Swimmer et al. 1988). Moreover, they suggest—on the basis, inter alia, of a reinterpretation of the aforementioned Hurlburt, Happen & Frith's (1994) data—that there is some evidence of a double dissociation between schizophrenic and autistic subjects: the MMs might be intact in autistics despite their impairment in third-person mindreading; in schizophrenics the pattern might be reversed. The MM theory provides a neo-Cartesian reply to TT—and especially to its eliminative implications since the mentalistic self-attributions based on MMs are immune to the potentially distorting influence of our intuitive theory of psychology. However, the MM theory faces at least two difficulties. To start with, the theory must tell us how MM establishes which attitude type (or percept type) a given mental state belongs to (Goldman 2006: 238-9). A possibility is that there is a separate MM for each propositional attitude type and for each perceptual modality. But then, as Engelbart and Carruthers (2010: 246) remark, since any MM can be selectively impaired, the MM theory predicts a multitude of dissociations—for example, subjects who can self-attribute beliefs but not desires, or visual experiences but not auditory ones, and so on. However, the hypothesis of such a massive disposability has little empirical plausibility.

Moreover, Carruthers (2011) has offered a book-length argument against the idea of a direct access to propositional attitudes. His neurocognitive framework is Bernard Bars' Global Workspace Theory model of consciousness (see Gennaro 2005: §4c), in which a range of perceptual systems "broadcast" their outputs (for example, sensory data from the environment, imagery, somatosensory and proprioceptive data) to a complex of conceptual systems (judgment-forming, memory-forming, desire-forming, decision-making systems, and so forth). Among the conceptual systems there is also a multi-componential "mindreading system," which generates higher-order judgments about the mental states of others and of oneself. By virtue of receiving globally broadcast perceptual states as input, the mindreading system can easily recognize those precepts, generating self-attributions of the form "I see something red," "It hurts," and so on. But the system receives no input from the systems that generate propositional attitude events (like judging and deciding). Consequently, the mindreading system cannot directly self-attribute propositional attitude events; it must infer them by exploiting the perceptual input (together with the outputs of various memory systems). Thus, Carruthers (2009: 124) concludes, "self-attributions of propositional attitude events like judging and deciding are always the result of a swift (and unconscious) process of self-interpretation." On this perspective, therefore, we do not introspect our own propositional attitude events. Our only form of access to those events is via self-interpretation, turning our mindreading faculty upon ourselves and engaging in unconscious interpretation of our own behaviour, physical circumstances, and sensory events like visual imagery and inner speech. Carruthers bases his proposal on considerations to do with the evolution of mindreading and metacognition, the rejection of the above-cited data that according to Nichols & Stich (2003) suggest developmental asynchronies and dissociation between self-attribution and other-attribution, and on evidence about the confabulation of attitudes. Thus, Carruthers develops a very sophisticated version of the symmetrical account of self-knowledge in which the theory-driven mechanisms underlying first- and third-person mindreading can count not only on observations and recollections of one's own behaviour and the circumstances in which it occurs/occurred, but also on the recognition of a multitude of perceptual and quasi-perceptual events.

2. Simulation-Theory

Until the mid-1980s the debate on the nature of mindreading was a debate between the different variants of TT. But in 1986, TT was impugned by Robert Gordon and, independently, by Jane Heal, who gave life to an alternative which was termed "simulation-theory" (ST). In 1989 Alvin Goldman and Paul Harris began to contribute to this new approach to mindreading. In 2006, Goldman provided the most thoroughly developed, empirically supported defines of a simulations account of our mentalistic abilities. According to ST, our third-person mindreading ability does not consist in implicit theorizing but rather in representing the psychological states and processes of others by mentally simulating them, that is, attempting to generate similar states and processes in ourselves. Thus, the same resources that are used in our own psychological states and processes are recycled—usually but not only in imagination—to provide an understanding of psychological states and processes of the simulated target. This has often been compared to the method of Einfühlung exalted by the theorists of Verstehen (see Stieber 2006: 5-19). For a mind reader to engage in this process of imaginative recycling, various information processing mechanisms are needed. The mind reader simulates the psychological ethology of the actions of the target in essentially two steps. First, the simulator generates pretend or imaginary mental states in her own mind which are intended to (at least partly) correspond to those of the target. Second, the simulator feeds the imaginary states into a suitable cognitive mechanism (for example, the decision-making system) that is taken "offline," that is, it is disengaged from the motor control systems. If the simulator's decision-making system is similar to the target's one, and the pretend mental states that the simulator introduces into the decision-making system (at least partly) match the target's, then the output of the simulator's decision-making system might reliably be attributed or assigned to the target. On this perspective, there is no need for an internally represented knowledge base and there is no need of a naïve theory of psychology. The simulator exploits a part of her cognitive apparatus as a model for a part of the simulated agent's cognitive apparatus. Hence follows one of the main advantages ST is supposed to have over TT—namely its computational parsimony. According to advocates of ST, the body of tacit folk-psychological knowledge which TT attributes to mind readers imposes too heavy a burden on mental computation. However, such a load will diminish radically if, instead of computing the body of knowledge posited by TT, mind readers must only co-opt mechanisms that are primarily used online, when they experience a kind of mental state, to run offline simulations of similar states in the target (the argument is suggested by Gordon 1986 and Goldman 1995, and challenged by Stich & Nichols 1992, 1995).

In the early years of the debate over ST, a focus was on its implications for the controversy between intentional realism and eliminative materialism. Gordon (1986) and Goldman (1989) suggested that by rejecting the assumption that folk psychology is a theory, ST undercuts eliminative. Stich & Ravenscroft (1994: §5), however, objected that ST undermines eliminative only provided that the latter adopts the sub personal version of TT. For ST does not deny the evident fact that human beings have intuitions about the mental, and neither rules out that such intuitions might be systematized by building, as David Lewis suggests, a theory that implies them. Consequently, ST does not refute eliminative; it instead forces the eliminative to include among the premises of her argument Lewis' personal formulation of TT, together with the observation/prediction that the theory implicit in our everyday talk about mental states is or will turn out to be seriously defective. One of the main objections that theory-theorists raise against ST is the argument from systematic errors in prediction. According to ST errors in prediction can arise either (i) because the predictor's executive system is different from that of the target, or (ii) because the pretend mental states that the predictor has introduced into the executive system do not match the ones that actually motivate the target. However, Stich & Nichols (1992, 1995; see also Nichols et al. 1996) describe experimental situations in which the participants systematically fail to predict the behaviour of targets, and in which it is unlikely that (I) or (ii) is the source of problem. Now, TT can easily explain such systematic errors in prediction: it is sufficient to assume that our naïve theory of psychology lacks the resources required to account for such situations. It is no surprise that a folk theory that is incomplete, partial, and in many cases seriously defective often causes predictive failures. But this option is obviously not available for ST: simulation-driven predictions are "cognitively impenetrable," that is, they are not affected by the predictor's knowledge or ignorance about psychological processes (see also Saxe 2005; and the replies by Gordon 2005 and Goldman 2006: 173-4). More recently, however, a consensus seems to be emerging to the effect that mindreading involves both TT and ST. For example, Goldman (2006) grants a variety of possible roles for theorizing in the context of what he calls "high-level mindreading." This is the imaginative simulation discussed so far, which is subject to voluntary control, is accessible to consciousness, and involves the ascription of complex mental states such as propositional attitudes. High-level simulation is a species of what Goldman terms "enactment imagination" (a notion that builds on Currie & Ravenscroft's 2002 concept of "recreative imagination"). Goldman contrasts high-level mindreading to the "low-level mindreading," which is unconscious, hard-wired, involves the attribution of structurally simple mental states such as face-based emotions (for example, joy, fear, disgust), and relies on simple imitative or mirroring processes (see, for example, Goldman & Shripad 2005). Now, theory plays a role in high-level mindreading. In a prediction task, for example, theory may be involved in the selection of the imaginary inputs that will be introduced into the executive system. In this case, Goldman (2006: 44) admits, mindreading depends on the cooperation of simulation and theorizing mechanisms. Goldman's blend of ST and TT (albeit with a strong emphasis on the simulative component) is not the only "hybrid" account of mindreading: for other hybrid approaches, see Cotterill & Carruthers (1999), Nichols & Stich (2003), and Penner & Muhlberger (2006). And it is right to say that now the debate aims first to establish to what extent and in which processes theory or simulation prevails. a. Simulation with and without Introspection There is an aspect, however, that makes Goldman's (2006) account of ST different from other hybrid theories of mindreading, namely the neo-Cartesian priority that he assigns to introspection. On his view, first-person mindreading both ontogenetically precedes and grounds third-person mindreading. Mind readers need to introspectively access their offline products of simulation before they can project them onto the target. And this, Goldman claims, is a form of "direct access." In 1993 Goldman put forward a phenomenological version of the inside access view (see above, §1c), by arguing that introspection is a process of detection and classification of one's (current) psychological states that does not depend at all on theoretical knowledge, but rather occurs in virtue of information about the phenomenological properties of such states.

But considering criticism (Carruthers 1996; Nichols & Stich 2003), in his 2006 book Goldman has remarkably reappraised the relevance of the qualitative component for the detection of psychological states, pointing out the centrality of the neural properties. Building on Craig's (2002) account of interception, as well as Marr's and Biederman's computational models of visual object recognition, Goldman now maintains that introspection is a perception-like process that involves a transduction mechanism that takes neural properties of mental states as input and outputs representations in a proprietary code (the introspective code, or the "I-code"). The I-code represents types of mental categories and classifies mental-state tokens in terms of those categories. Goldman also suggests some possible primitives of the I-code. So, for example, our coding of the concept of pain might be the combination of the "bodily feeling" parameter (a certain raw feeling) with the "preference" or "valence" one (a negative valence toward the feeling). Thus, the neural version of the inside access view is an attempt to solve the problem of the recognition of the attitude type, which proved problematic for Nichols and Stich's representationalism-functionalist approach (see above, §1c). However, since different percept and attitude types are presumably realized in different cerebral areas, each percept or attitude type will depend on a specific informational channel to feed the introspective mechanism. Consequently, Goldman's theory also seems to be open to the objection of massive disposability raised to the MM theory (see Engelbart and Carruthers 2010: 247). Goldman's primacy of first-person mindreading is, however, rejected by other situationists. According to Gordon's (1995, 1996) "radical" version of ST, simulation can occur without introspective access to one's own mental states. The simulative process begins not with my pretending to be the target, but rather with my becoming the target. As Gordon (1995: 54) puts it, simulation is not "a transfer but a transformation." "I" changes its referent and the equivalence "I=target" is established. In virtue of this de-rigidification of the personal pronoun, any introspective step is ruled out: one does not first assign a psychological state to oneself to transfer it to the target. Since the simulator becomes the target, no analogical inference from oneself to the other is needed. Still more radically, simulation can occur without having any mentalistic concepts. Our basic competence in the use of utterances of the form "I <propositional attitude> that p" involves not direct access to the propositional attitudes, but only an "ascent routine" through which we express our propositional attitudes in this new linguistic form (see Gordon 2007). Carruthers has raised two objections to Gordon's radical ST. First, it is a "step back" to a form of "quasi-behaviourism" (Carruthers 1996: 38). Second, Gordon problematically assumes that our mentalistic abilities are constituted by language (Carruthers 2011: 225-27). In developmental psychology de Villiers & de Villiers (2003) have put forward a constitution-thesis like Gordon's: thinking about mental states comes from internalizing the language with which these states are expressed in the child's linguistic environment. More specifically, mastery of the grammatical rules for embedding tensed complement clauses under verbs of speech or cognition provides children with a necessary representational format for dealing with false beliefs. However, correlation between linguistic exposure and mindreading does not depend on the use of specific grammatical structures. In a training study Lohman & Tomaselli (2003) found that performance on a false-belief task is enhanced by simply using perspective-shifting discourse, without any use of sentential complement syntax. Moreover, syntax is not constitutive of the mentalistic capacities of adults. Varley et al. (2001) and Dapperly et al. (2006) provided clear evidence that adults with profound grammatical impairment show no impairments on non-verbal tests of mindreading.

Finally, mastery of sentence complements is not even a necessary condition of the development of mindreading in children. Penner et al. (2005) have shown that such mastery may be required for statements about beliefs but not about desires (as in English), for beliefs and desires (as in German), or for neither beliefs nor desires (Chinese); and yet children who learn each of these three languages all understand and talk about desire significantly earlier than belief.

b. Simulation in Low-Level Mindreading Another argument for a (prevalently) simulations approach to mindreading consists in pointing out that TT is thoroughly limited to high-level mindreading (essentially the attribution of propositional attitudes), whereas ST is also well equipped to account for forms of low-level mindreading such as the perception of emotions or the recognition of facial expressions and motor intentions (see Slurs & Macdonald 2008: 155).

This claim finds its main support in the interplay between ST and neuroscience. In the early 1990s mirror neurons were first described in the ventral premotor cortex and inferior parietal lobe of macaque monkeys. These visuomotor neurons activate not only when the monkey executes motor acts (such as grasping, manipulating, holding, and tearing objects), but also when it observes the same, or similar, acts performed by the experimenter or a conspecific. Although there is only one study that seems to offer direct evidence for the existence of mirror neurons in humans (Mikael et al. 2010), many neurophysiological and brain imaging investigations support the existence of a human action mirroring system. For example, fMRI studies using action observation or imitation tasks demonstrated activation in areas in the human ventral premotor and parietal cortices assumed to be homologous to the areas in the monkey cortex containing mirror neurons (see Pizzolatto et al. 2002). It should be emphasized that most of the mirror neurons that discharge when a certain type of motor act is performed also activate when the same act is perceived, even though it is not performed with the same physical movement—for example, many mirror neurons that discharge when the monkey grasps food with the hand also activate when it sees a conspecific who grasps food with the mouth. This seems to suggest that mirror neurons code or represent an action at a high level of abstraction, that is, they are receptive not only to a mere movement but indeed to an action. In 1998, Vittorio Gales and Goldman wrote a very influential article in which mirror neurons were indicated as the basis of the simulative process. When the mirror neurons in the simulator's brain are externally activated in observation mode, their activity matches (simulates or resonates with) that of mirror neurons in the target's brain, and this resonance process reproductively outputs a representation of the target's intention from a perception of her movement. More recently several objections have been raised against the "resonance" ST advocated by some researchers that have built on Gales and Goldman's hypothesis. Some critics, although admitting the presence of mirror neurons in both non-human and human primates, have drastically reappraised their role in mindreading. For example, Saxe (2009) has argued that there is no evidence that mirror neurons represent the internal states of the target rather than some relatively abstract properties of observed actions (see also Jacob & Jeanne rod 2005; Jacob 2008). On the other hand, Goldman himself has mitigated his original position. Unlike Gales, Keysets & Pizzolatto (2004), who propose mirror systems as the unifying basis of all social cognition, now Goldman (2006) considers mirror neuron activity, or motor resonance in general, as merely a possible part of low-level mindreading. Nonetheless, it is right to say that resonance phenomena are at the forefront of the field of social neuroscience (see Slurs & Macdonald 2008: 156).

3. Social Cognition without Mindreading

By the early 21st century, the primacy that both TT and ST assigns to mindreading in social cognition had been challenged. One line of attack has come from philosophers working in the phenomenological tradition, such as Shaun Gallagher, Matthew Ratcliffe, and Dan Zehavi (see Gallagher & Zehavi 2008). Others working more from the analytic tradition, such as Jose Luis Bermudez (2005, 2006b), Dan Hutto (2008), and Heidi Meibum (2003, 2007) have made similar points. Let's focus on Bermudez' contribution because he offers a very clear account of the kind of cognitive mechanisms that might sub serve forms of social understanding and coordination without mindreading (for a brief overview of this literature, see Slurs & Macdonald 2008; for an exhaustive examination, see Hersch Bach 2010).

Bermudez (2005) argues that the role of high-level mindreading in social cognition needs to be drastically re-evaluated. We must rethink the traditional nexus between intelligent behaviour and propositional attitudes, realizing that much social understanding and social coordination are sub served by mechanisms that do not capitalize on the machinery of intentional psychology. For example, a mechanism of emotional sensitivity such as "social referencing" is a form of low-level mindreading that sub serve social understanding and social coordination without involving the attribution of propositional attitudes (see Bermudez 2006a: 55). To this point Bermudez is on the same wavelength as situationists and social neuroscientists in drawing our attention to forms of low-level mindreading that have been largely neglected by philosophers. However, Bermudez goes a step beyond them and explores cases of social interactions that point in a different direction, that is, situations that involve mechanisms that can no longer be described as mindreading mechanisms. He offers two examples.

(1) In game theory there are social interactions that are modelled without assuming that the agents involved are engaged in explaining or predicting each other's behaviour. In social situations that have the structure of the iterated prisoner's dilemma, the so-called "tit-for-tat" heuristic simply says: "start out cooperating and then mirror your partner's move for each successive move" (Axelrod 1984). Applying this heuristic simply requires understanding the moves available to each player (cooperation or defection) and remembering what happened in the last round. So, we have here a case of social interaction that is conducted based on a heuristic strategy that looks backward to the results of previous interactions rather than to their psychological ethology. We do not need to infer other players' reasons; we only must coordinate our behaviour with theirs. (2) There is another important class of social interactions that involve our predicting and/or explaining the actions of other participants, but in which the relevant predictions and explanations seem to proceed without us having to attribute propositional attitudes. These social interactions rest on what social psychologists call "scripts" ("frames" in artificial intelligence), that is, complex information structures that allow predictions to be made on the basis of the specification of the purpose of some social practice (for example, eating a meal at a restaurant), the various individual roles, and the appropriate sequence of moves. According to Bermudez, then, much social interaction is enabled by a suite of relatively simple mechanisms that exploit purely behavioural regularities. It is important to notice that these mechanisms sub serve central social cognition (in Feodor's sense). Nevertheless, they implement relatively simple processes of template matching and pattern recognition, that is, processes that are paradigmatic cases of perceptual processing. For example, when a player A applies the tit-for-tat rule, A must determine what the other player B did in the preceding round. This can be implemented in virtue of a template matching in which A verifies that B's behavioural pattern matches A's prototype of cooperation and defection. And also detecting the social roles implicated in a script-based interaction is a case

of template matching: one verifies whether the perceived behaviour matches one of the templates associated with the script (or the prototype represented in the "frame"). Bermudez (2005: 223) notes that the idea that much of what we intuitively identify as central processing is actually implemented by mechanisms of template matching and pattern recognition has been repeatedly put forward by the advocates of the connectionist computationalism, especially by Paul M. Churchland. But unlike the latter, Bermudez does not carry the reappraisal of the role of propositional attitudes in social cognition to the point of their elimination; he argues that social cognition does not involve high-level mindreading when the social world is "transparent" or "ready-to-hand," as he says quoting Heidegger's zander. However, when we find ourselves in social situations that are "opaque," that is, situations in which all the standard mechanisms of social understanding and interpersonal negotiation break down, it seems that we cannot help but appeal to the type of metarepresentational thinking characteristic of intentional psychology (2005: 205-6).

Meaning of Human Mind:

Human Mind is the sum-total of various mental processes such as observing, knowing, thinking, reasoning, feeling, wishing, imagining, remembering, judging and others. It is not a separate object which has or possesses these mental processes. Mind is these mental processes. If we take away these mental processes. No mind is left, just as no chair is left if we take away its back, seat, arms, and legs. Therefore, mind is another name for those mental processes and activities put together.

Our Human mind grows just as our body grows. It becomes more complex with advancing years. In other words, our mental processes become richer and more complicated day by day. For example, there is a difference between thinking and reasoning of an adult and those of a child of three years. The human mind is not only the sum-total of all conscious mental processes, as it was believed earlier; it includes preconscious and unconscious processes, as well. It must be noted, however, that mind is one and is a unity. There are three levels at which it functions. At one level, we are aware of our mental processes; this is the 'conscious'.

At another level, we are not conscious of our mental processes; this gives us the "unconscious', still at another level, we are not aware of our mental processes at a certain time, but we were aware of them before, and can, again, be aware of them if we try. This is our preconscious.

The Unconscious:

The unconscious processes constitute the unconscious or the unconscious mind. It is the processes of which we are incapable of becoming conscious unless special methods of psychoanalysis are used. These processes lie buried deep down in the hidden recesses of our mind, very much below the level of consciousness.

It was Freud and his earliest followers Jung and Adler who strongly advocated the existence of the unconscious which could be understood and known through psycho-analysis – a method of unearthing and analysing the unconscious. Due to the discovery of the unconscious, our knowledge of the human mind is very much extended.

These thinkers have told us that the unconscious includes all forgotten past experiences, our repressed wishes and desires, our fears, and phobias for which we do not know the reason, or our eccentric likes and dislikes. Many of these unconscious mental processes appear in and cause our dreams, slips of pen or tongue. They cause abnormal behaviour in the form of neuroses and psychoses.

It must be noted that there are no pigeon-holes or compartments in our mind which store the pre-conscious or unconscious processes separately. The preconscious and unconscious are a part of the same mind to which the conscious processes belong. The former are simply those mental processes which we have forgotten, either temporarily or permanently. Their connections with our conscious process are broken for the time being.

These are as follows:

(I) Freud refers to the unconscious, the preconscious and the conscious as the topographical aspects of the mind or self or psyche. For him, the unconscious is of paramount importance. It is the true psychic reality. The conscious is only a fraction when compared with the vast unconscious. In it are stored and found millions of infantile wishes, unsatisfied desires, cravings, and urges, many of which are legacies from childhood.

Freud proves the existence of the unconscious by referring to many phenomena such as our experiences that we cannot recall, the phenomenon of somnambulism, post-hypnotic suggestion, dreams, morbid forgetfulness and slips of pen and tongue.

(ii) The second tenet of this system is the dynamic aspects of mind the – Id, the Ego, and the Super ego. Freud believed that all behaviour is the resultant of the dynamic conflicts between the forces of the Id, the Ego, and the Superego at the conscious, and unconscious levels of mind. The Id is the primitive undifferentiated basis of the whole human mind. It is completely dominated by the pleasure principle. It has no idea of time or reality. Its strivings are originally impulsive and uncontrolled out they are controlled by society and the reality principle during development.

The Ego represents the self or the conscious intelligence. It is the integrating part of the personality. It is an adjuster between the wishes of the Id on the one hand and the demands of external reality on the other. It must face the three sets of forces e.g., external reality, the instinctive pressure from the Id and inhibition or control from the Superego.

The Superego is the chief force that makes for the socialisation of the individual. It is primarily sociologically and culturally conditioned. It corresponds to the idea of conscience. It represents the social and moral ideal which society sets up for our behaviour. Within it reside the forces of repression and censorship, self-observation, and self-criticism. Mitchell says, 'By means of identification with the parents or one of the parents and Ego-ideal is set up within the Ego, and as a Superego, adopts and critical and condemnatory attitude of the parents towards the libidinal impulses.

(iii) The third tenet of psychoanalysis is that of conflict, repression, and complexes. As said above, according to Freud, all behaviour is the resultant of the dynamic conflicts between the forces of the Id, the Ego, and the Super-ego. The Id impulses which are largely sexual and aggressive in nature want to be satisfied, but these come in conflict with the Ego and the Super-ego. In other words, there is a clash between the primitive impulses and social and moral taboos, prohibitions, and obstructions. Our conflicts may be conscious or unconscious. When we are aware of the conflict and sources causing it, the conflict is at the conscious level. But there are times when we are not aware of the real motives causing conflict. We experience feelings of strain, stress, and anxiety but why? We cannot easily tell. The motivations of the conflict are unconscious. We are not aware of them. This is the end psychic or unconscious conflict.

This is how it happens. The conflict even at the conscious level, is a painful affair which creates tension in the human mind. It should end as soon as possible. It can be ended by following the Id impulses and by ignoring the claims of the Ego and the Super-ego or the external world. It can be ended by consciously denying the impulses or urges completely and following the demands of the Ego or Super-ego.

Another method of ending the conflicts is by throwing those impulses into allied channels sanctioned by society and thus obtaining for them a vicarious satisfaction. For example, many women who do not marry, satisfy a fundamental wish by becoming nurses or by directing their own energies to the care and welfare of children. But most people follow neither of these courses, it is very difficult to endure the ideas of defeat which result from the denial or our Id, desires.

Again, the Id impulses cannot be satisfied in the face of social opposition. Even throwing them into other social sanctioned channels is not an easy task. We need suitable potentialities, education, guidance, and environment for that. Normally, the conflict is resolved or ended, in an average individual, by an actual forcing down of these wishes into the unconscious.

This unconscious forgetfulness of the Id impulses or throwing down of these impulses into the unconscious is called repression. Thus, "what is unpleasant obnoxious, embarrassing or offensive is vanished from consciousness". With repression, the conflict shifts from the conscious into the unconscious.

These repressed wishes or desires remain active in the unconscious regions of our mind. They slowly gather strength by making alliance with other allied repressed experiences, thus forming an active group. This group of repressed desires working with a common end, i.e. to come back to the level of consciousness, is called a complex. As soon as complexes are formed, they give rise to a conflict in the unconscious, known as the endocyclic conflict. These complexes are just like exiles whose presence back in the conscious is not tolerated. But they do strive to regain consciousness. The forces of the Ego and Super-ego would not permit this. If they come back to the conscious, they would again create conflict and tension.

The mental force that keeps the repressed undesirable wishes confined to the unconscious is technically known as the censor. The censor is not an outside agency implanted in us but is a part of our own personality. It represents the moral and social aspects of the Ego and Super-ego.

But the censor is always not uniformly vigilant, its activities are considerably weakened during sleep as also during such moments that the repressed wishes seek to regain consciousness. At times, they may come in mask or in disguise and thus elude the vigilance of the censor. Such disguise may take the form of dreams, slips of pen and tongue, forgetfulness, mannerism of speech and others.

Sometimes, they may manifest themselves in mental mechanisms such as transference, projection identification, rationalization, and others. The complexes may also cause neurotic disturbances or psychotic disorders of various types.

(iv) The fourth principle of psychoanalysis is Freud's theory of instinct and libido. According to him, there are two decidedly inmates' psychological urges or instincts. These urges may be called 'Eros' of life or love instinct and Thanatos or the death instincts or aggression. They work through the existing structure of a person's being in his environment and determine what he is and what he does.

They are modified by the life experience of the individual, particularly those of the earliest years of life. These instincts are not opposed and mutually independent forces. They fuse and intermix. The intermixture of the two instincts leads to the Freudian principle of ambivalence loving and hating the same person.

Libido is the energy that works throughout the whole psychic system the energy of the life instinct. It is the source of sexual love, self-love, parental affection, friendship and of love for humanity in general. It causes the infantile sex-life; when the libido flows outward, it causes object-love; when it flows inward, it causes self-love or narcissism.

(v) The fifth tenet of the psycho-analytical theory is the principle of psycho- sexual genesis or infantile sexuality. Sexual life, according to Freud, does not start at puberty. Its first manifestations may be clearly seen after birth. Sexuality embraces many activities which have no connection with genitals. The fundamental functions of sexuality are to obtain pleasure from zones of the body. During the infancy and childhood period, this sexuality has three phases (a) oral, (b) anal-sadistic and (c) phallic.

At first the child derives libidinal satisfaction from the mouth; at three or four this pleasure is given by anal movement. After this we have the phallic phase when the child evinces interest in his genitalia. It is in this phase when the development of the Oedipus Complex takes place. The libido is directed towards an external love object of the opposite sex.

The latency period (5 to 12 years) is essentially one of psychic consolidation and synthesis. The psyche has a respite from infantile urges and the Super-ego develops. The pubertal period extends from 12 years onwards. There is a revival of sexuality and its passes through auto-erotic and homosexual phases before it is allowed its normal outlet in heterosexual behaviour.

Meaning of Human Mind:

Human Mind is the sum-total of various mental processes such as observing, knowing, thinking, reasoning, feeling, wishing, imagining, remembering, judging and others. It is not a separate object which has or possesses these mental processes. Mind is these mental processes. If we take away these mental processes. No mind is left, just as no chair is left if we take away its back, seat, arms, and legs. Therefore, mind is another name for those mental processes and activities put together. Our Human mind grows just as our body grows. It becomes more complex with advancing years. In other words, our mental processes become richer and more complicated day by day. For example, there is a difference between thinking and reasoning of an adult and those of a child of three years. The human mind is not only the sum-total of all conscious mental processes, as it was believed earlier; it includes preconscious and unconscious processes, as well. It must be noted, however, that mind is one and is a unity. There are three levels at which it functions. At one level, we are aware of our mental processes; this is the 'conscious'. At another level, we are not conscious of our mental processes; this gives us the "unconscious', still at another level, we are not aware of our mental processes at a certain time, but we were aware of them before, and can, again, be aware of them if we try. This is our preconscious. The Unconscious:

The unconscious processes constitute the unconscious or the unconscious mind. It is the processes of which we are incapable of becoming conscious unless special methods of psychoanalysis are used. These processes lie buried deep down in the hidden recesses of our mind, very much below the level of consciousness. It was Freud and his earliest followers Jung and Adler who strongly advocated the existence of the unconscious which could be understood and known through psycho-analysis – a method of unearthing and analysing the unconscious. Due to the discovery of the unconscious, our knowledge of the human mind is very much extended. These thinkers have told us that the unconscious includes all forgotten past experiences, our repressed wishes and desires, our fears, and phobias for which we do not know the reason, or our eccentric likes and dislikes. Many of these unconscious mental processes appear in and cause our dreams, slips of pen or tongue. They cause abnormal behaviour in the form of neuroses and psychoses. It must be noted that there are no pigeon-holes or compartments in our mind which store the pre-conscious or unconscious processes separately. The preconscious and unconscious are a part of the same mind to which the conscious processes belong. The former are simply those mental processes which we have forgotten, either temporarily or permanently. Their connections with our conscious process are broken for the time being.

These are as follows: (I) Freud refers to the unconscious, the preconscious and the conscious as the topographical aspects of the mind or self or psyche. For him, the unconscious is of paramount importance. It is the true psychic reality. The conscious is only a fraction when compared with the vast unconscious. In it are stored and found millions of infantile wishes, unsatisfied desires, cravings, and urges, many of which are legacies from childhood. Freud proves the existence of the unconscious by referring to many phenomena such as our experiences that we cannot recall, the phenomenon of somnambulism, post-hypnotic suggestion, dreams, morbid forgetfulness and slips of pen and tongue. (ii) The second tenet of this system is the dynamic aspects of mind the – Id, the Ego, and the Super ego. Freud believed that all behaviour is the resultant of the dynamic conflicts between the forces of the Id, the Ego, and the Superego at the conscious, and unconscious levels of mind. The Id is the primitive undifferentiated basis of the whole human mind. It is completely dominated by the pleasure principle. It has no idea of time or reality. Its strivings are originally impulsive and uncontrolled out they are controlled by society and the reality principle during development. Structure of the Mind the Ego represents the self or the conscious intelligence. It is the integrating part of the personality. It is an adjuster between the wishes of the Id on the one hand and the demands of external reality on the other. It must face the three sets of forces e.g., external reality, the instinctive pressure from the Id and inhibition or control from the Superego. The Superego is the chief force that makes for the socialisation of the individual. It is primarily sociologically and culturally conditioned. It corresponds to the idea of conscience. It represents the social and moral ideal which society sets up for our behaviour. Within it reside the forces of repression and censorship, self-observation, and self-criticism. Mitchell says, 'By means of identification with the parents or one of the parents and Ego-ideal is set up within the Ego, and as a Superego, adopts and critical and condemnatory attitude of the parents towards the libidinal impulses. (iii) The third tenet of psychoanalysis is that of conflict, repression, and complexes. As said above, according to Freud, all behaviour is the resultant of the dynamic conflicts between the forces of the Id, the Ego, and the Super-ego. The Id impulses which are largely sexual and aggressive in nature want to be satisfied, but these come in conflict with the Ego and the Super-ego. In other words, there is a clash between the primitive impulses and social and moral taboos, prohibitions, and obstructions. Our conflicts may be conscious or unconscious. When we are aware of the conflict and sources causing it, the conflict is at the conscious level. But there are times when we are not aware of the real motives causing conflict. We experience feelings of strain, stress, and anxiety but why? We cannot easily tell. The motivations of the conflict are unconscious. We are not aware of them. This is the end psychic or unconscious conflict. This is how it happens. The conflict even at the conscious level, is a painful affair which creates tension in the human mind. It should end as soon as possible. It can be ended by following the Id impulses and by ignoring the claims of the Ego and the Super-ego or the external world. It can be ended by consciously denying the impulses or urges completely and following the demands of the Ego or Super-ego. Another method of ending the conflicts is by throwing those impulses into allied channels sanctioned by society and thus obtaining for them a vicarious satisfaction. For example, many women who do not marry, satisfy a fundamental wish by becoming nurses or by directing their own energies to the care and welfare of children. But most people follow neither of these courses, it is very difficult to endure the ideas of defeat which result from the denial or our Id, desires. Again, the Id impulses cannot be satisfied in the face of social opposition. Even throwing them into other social sanctioned channels is not an easy task. We need suitable potentialities, education, guidance, and environment for that. Normally, the conflict is resolved or ended, in an average individual, by an actual forcing down of these wishes into the unconscious. This unconscious forgetfulness of the Id impulses or throwing down of these impulses into the unconscious is called repression. Thus, "what is unpleasant obnoxious, embarrassing or offensive is vanished from consciousness". With repression, the conflict shifts from the conscious into the unconscious. These repressed wishes or desires remain active in the unconscious regions of our mind. They slowly gather strength by making alliance with other allied repressed experiences, thus forming an active group. This group of repressed desires working with a common end, i.e. to come back to the level of consciousness, is called a complex. As soon as complexes are formed, they give rise to a conflict in the unconscious, known as the endocyclic conflict. Structure of the Human Mind Compared to an Iceberg These complexes are just like exiles whose presence back in the conscious is not tolerated. But they do strive to regain consciousness. The forces of the Ego and Super-ego would not permit this. If they come back to the conscious, they would again create conflict and tension. The mental force that keeps the repressed undesirable wishes confined to the unconscious is technically known as the censor. The censor is not an outside agency implanted in us but is a part of our own personality. It represents the moral and social aspects of the Ego and Super-ego. But the censor is always not uniformly vigilant, its activities are considerably weakened during sleep as also during such moments that the repressed wishes seek to regain consciousness. At times, they may come in mask or in disguise and thus elude the vigilance of the censor. Such disguise may take the form of dreams, slips of pen and tongue, forgetfulness, mannerism of speech and others. Sometimes, they may manifest themselves in mental mechanisms such as transference, projection identification, rationalization, and others. The complexes may also cause neurotic disturbances or psychotic disorders of various types. (iv) The fourth principle of psychoanalysis is Freud's theory of instinct and libido. According to him, there are two decidedly inmates' psychological urges or instincts. These urges may be called 'Eros' of life or love instinct and Thanatos or the death instincts or aggression. They work through the existing structure of a person's being in his environment and determine what he is and what he does. They are modified by the life experience of the individual, particularly those of the earliest years of life. These instincts are not opposed and mutually independent forces. They fuse and intermix. The intermixture of the two instincts leads to the Freudian principle of ambivalence loving and hating the same person. Libido is the energy that works throughout the whole psychic system the energy of the life instinct. It is the source of sexual love, self-love, parental affection, friendship and of love for humanity in general. It causes the infantile sex-life; when the libido flows outward, it causes object-love; when it flows inward, it causes self-love or narcissism. (v) The fifth tenet of the psycho-analytical theory is the principle of psycho- sexual genesis or infantile sexuality. Sexual life, according to Freud, does not start at puberty. Its first manifestations may be clearly seen after birth. Sexuality embraces many activities which have no connection with genitals. The fundamental functions of sexuality are to obtain pleasure from zones of the body. During the infancy and childhood period, this sexuality has three phases (a) oral, (b) anal-sadistic and (c) phallic. At first the child derives libidinal satisfaction from the mouth; at three or four this pleasure is given by anal movement. After this we have the phallic phase when the child evinces interest in his genitalia. It is in this phase when the development of the Oedipus Complex takes place. The libido is directed towards an external love object of the opposite sex. The latency period (5 to 12 years) is essentially one of psychic consolidation and synthesis. The psyche has a respite from infantile urges and the Super-ego develops. The pubertal period extends from 12 years onwards. There is a revival of sexuality and its passes through auto-erotic and homosexual phases before it is allowed its normal outlet in heterosexual behaviour. Mind power is one of the strongest and most useful powers you possess.

This power consists of your thoughts.

The thoughts that pass through your mind are responsible for everything that happens in your life. Your predominant thoughts influence your behaviour and attitude and control your actions and reactions. As your thoughts are, so is your life. Be careful of what you think

Thoughts are like a video that plays on the screen of your mind. What you play there, determines the kind of life you live and the experiences you meet. To make changes in your life, you must play a different video, one that you like more. The Power of Thoughts Is a Creative Power

You can train and strengthen this power. You can use it to make changes in your life, and to influence other people's minds. If you plant seeds, water them, and give them fertilizers, they will grow into healthy and strong plants. Thoughts, like seeds, have a natural tendency to grow and manifest in your life, if you feed them with attention, interest, and enthusiasm. Your thoughts pass from your conscious mind to your subconscious mind, which in turn, influences your actions in accordance with these thoughts. Your thoughts also pass to other minds, and consequently, people who can help you, might offer you their help, sometimes, without even knowing why. This might some strange and unbelievable. You don't have to accept these words, but if you analyse the kind of thoughts you think, and the kind of life you live, you will discover interesting things about the mind. The power of your mind is part of the creative power of the Universe, which means that your thoughts work together with it. You are a manifestation of the Universal mind. When you repeat the same thought over and again, in one way or another, this mighty power helps you make your thoughts come true. Using the power of thoughts effectively, is an act of "practical daydreaming". How to Use the Power of Your Thoughts? Visualize a perfect scene of whatever you want to accomplish.

Put a lot of detail, colour, sound, scent, and life into these mental scenes.

Repeat your visualization often, with faith and attention, and your subconscious will accept these mental scenes as real experiences. The subconscious mind does not distinguish between real and imaginary experiences and accepts both as real. It will start making changes and attracting opportunities, to make your reality match the images in your subconscious mind.

Actions, situations, and objects that you visualize frequently, eventually, manifest on the material plane in a natural way. This manifestation does not happen overnight. It needs time, and depends on how ambitious and sincere you are, and how much time and attention you put into this action. You can use this process to change negative habits and build new, positive habits or skills. You can also use it for attracting money and possessions, for promotion at work, for building a business, improving health and relationships, changing circumstances, and for practically almost everything. Pay attention to the thoughts you think. Do your best to reject negative thoughts, and to allow into your mind only thoughts that bring good, happy, and positive results.
The good news is that there are a number of different ways to improve your brain power, especially if you're willing to do some things consistently over a longer period of time. Let's explore eight ways that you can support your brain health.

1. Exercise.

We all know that we should be getting regular exercise. However, most entrepreneur lead busy, rushed lives, and can't always find the time to fit physical activity in. The trick might be to think of it in reverse: you can't afford not to exercise if you want to live a long, healthy, productive life. Exercise not only benefits your brain health and cognition; it can also improve your memory. In the long run, it can even protect your brain against degeneration. If that isn't reason enough to get into a regular workout routine, who knows what is? Related: Why Food, Sleep and Exercise Are Critical to Success 2. Drink coffee.

Many people start their days with a cup of coffee, and it turns out this ritual could benefit your cognitive functions in the short term. Caffeine, of course, helps to keep you alert. However, it can also help you to stay focused on repetitive and tedious tasks, and will even boost your intelligence, including your reaction time and reasoning. Obviously, the effects of coffee are not permanent. However, it can make your brain work more efficiently until that caffeine high wears off. 3. Get some sunlight.

Sunlight and exercise can sometimes go hand in hand. This mostly depends on what part of the world you live in; how much sunlight is available at different times of the year and how realistic it is for you to spend time in the outdoors. Getting too little sunlight is not good for your brain. Higher levels of vitamin D in your system allow you to perform better and can even slow down the aging of your brain. Too much sunlight can be bad for your skin, but if you aren't getting enough, your brain functions may suffer. Of course, you can always take vitamin D supplements if you find that you aren't able to get outside as much as you would like to. Just remember to take supplements in moderation.4. Build strong connections. It has often been said that the entrepreneurial journey is a lonely one. As it turns out, that may not be good for your cognitive functions. If you often feel lonely, it can result in psychological and cognitive decline, as these feelings can have a negative impact on your sleep, increase your blood pressure, contribute to depression, and even lower your overall well-being. Most entrepreneurs know how to communicate and build connections. The key thing is to build a strong support system around you, as that will enable you to stay healthy mentally and psychologically over the long term. 5. Meditate.

Meditation is a trending topic among many entrepreneurs right now, and its benefits are hard to argue with. Not only does meditation reduce your stress levels, it can also prevent age-related disorders such as Alzheimer's or dementia. This speaks to the importance of self-care. Taking a mere 10 to 15 minutes out of your day to practice meditation could extend your cognitive longevity and allow you to reduce your overall stress levels too. Related: Less Sleep

Makes You More Likely to Catch a Cold, Study Finds 6. Sleep well.

This can be another tricky area for entrepreneurs. Early mornings and late nights sometimes come with the territory, and the stresses or excitement that come with building and growing a business can have undesirable effects on sleep patterns. Sleep is required to consolidate memory and learning. If you don't get enough sleep, your Gray-matter volume in your frontal lobe may begin to decrease. Your frontal lobe supports and controls your working memory as well as executive function, making it particularly important. In short, if you don't get enough sleep, you'll have less brain in your head. 7. Eat well.

It shouldn't come as a surprise that nutrition plays a significant part in your brain health. Entrepreneurs are often rushing from one meeting to another, leaving themselves with very little or no time to eat well. You must focus on getting the right kind of nutrition. Antioxidants and amino acids are particularly important, and vitamin E can also be beneficial. Drinking wine is known to improve your cognitive function -- assuming you consume it in moderation -- and nuts, blueberries, whole grains, and avocados are also beneficial. What's good for your body also tends to be good for your brain. 8. Play Tetris. This might come to you as a bit of a surprise, but playing Tetris is known to have several positive effects on your brain. Playing Tetris will increase Gray matter for a short amount of time, and it can also help with performing spatially related tasks. The most interesting part is that playing Tetris after a traumatic experience can prevent your brain from solidifying those memories. That means fewer flashbacks to negative memories over the long haul. If you always have a smartphone or tablet with you, then incorporating a little bit of Tetris into your day should prove to be straightforward. Just don't get carried away and forget to work, too! Final thoughts More than anything else, improving your brain power is about habits, and habits take time to build. The best approach is to focus on one or two things at a time. Giving your life a complete makeover is going to prove much more challenging, and the habits you attempt to develop may not stick. This is counterproductive.

Not only is balance hard to achieve, often it never is in the life of an entrepreneur. However, constant experimentation and tweaking will allow you to test things out and see what works best for you. Have you ever had a fellow motorist stopped beside you at a red light, singing his brains out, or picking his nose, or otherwise behaving in ways he might not normally do in public? There is something about being alone in a car that encourages people to zone out and forget that others can see them. Although these little lapses of attention are amusing for the rest of us, they are also instructive when it comes to the topic of consciousness.

A young man sits behind the wheel of a car with his eyes closed as he sings along with the radio.

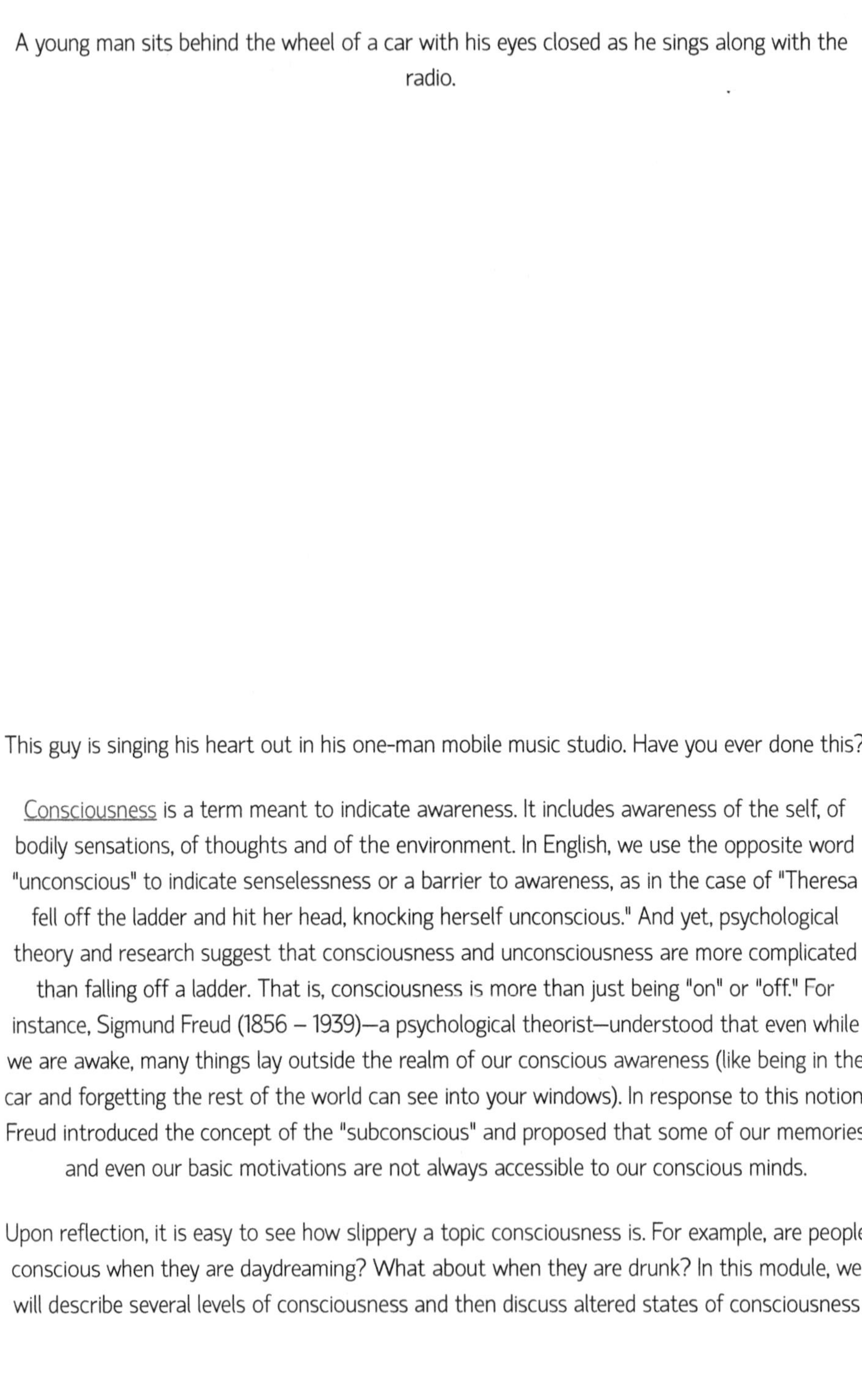

This guy is singing his heart out in his one-man mobile music studio. Have you ever done this?

Consciousness is a term meant to indicate awareness. It includes awareness of the self, of bodily sensations, of thoughts and of the environment. In English, we use the opposite word "unconscious" to indicate senselessness or a barrier to awareness, as in the case of "Theresa fell off the ladder and hit her head, knocking herself unconscious." And yet, psychological theory and research suggest that consciousness and unconsciousness are more complicated than falling off a ladder. That is, consciousness is more than just being "on" or "off." For instance, Sigmund Freud (1856 – 1939)—a psychological theorist—understood that even while we are awake, many things lay outside the realm of our conscious awareness (like being in the car and forgetting the rest of the world can see into your windows). In response to this notion, Freud introduced the concept of the "subconscious" and proposed that some of our memories and even our basic motivations are not always accessible to our conscious minds.

Upon reflection, it is easy to see how slippery a topic consciousness is. For example, are people conscious when they are daydreaming? What about when they are drunk? In this module, we will describe several levels of consciousness and then discuss altered states of consciousness such as hypnosis and sleep.

Levels of Awareness

In 1957, a marketing researcher inserted the words "Eat Popcorn" onto one frame of a film being shown across the United States. And although that frame was only projected onto the movie screen for 1/24th of a second—a speed too fast to be perceived by conscious awareness—the researcher reported an increase in popcorn sales by nearly 60%. Almost immediately, all forms of "subliminal messaging" were regulated in the US and banned in countries such as Australia and the United Kingdom. Even though it was later shown that the researcher had made up the data (he hadn't even inserted the words into the film), this fear about influences on our subconscious persists. At its heart, this issue pits various levels of awareness against one another. On the one hand, we have the "low awareness" of subtle, even subliminal influences. On the other hand, there is you—the conscious thinking, feeling you, which includes all that you are currently aware of, even reading this sentence. However, when we consider these different levels of awareness separately, we can better understand how they operate.

Low Awareness

You are constantly receiving and evaluating sensory information. Although each moment has too many sights, smells, and sounds for them all to be consciously considered, our brains are nonetheless processing all that information. For example, have you ever been at a party, overwhelmed by all the people and conversation, when out of nowhere you hear your name called? Even though you have no idea what else the person is saying, you are somehow conscious of your name (for more on this, "the cocktail party effect," see Nobu's Module on Attention). So, even though you may not be aware of various stimuli in your environment, your brain is paying closer attention than you think.

Similar to a reflex (like jumping when startled), some cues, or significant sensory information, will automatically elicit a response from us even though we never consciously perceive it. For example, Lohman and Soares measured subtle variations in sweating of participants with a fear of snakes. The researchers flashed pictures of different objects (e.g., mushrooms, flowers, and most importantly, snakes) on a screen in front of them, but did so at speeds that left the participant clueless as to what he or she had actually seen. However, when snake pictures were flashed, these participants started sweating more (i.e., a sign of fear), even though they had no idea what they'd just viewed!

Although our brains perceive some stimuli without our conscious awareness, do they really affect our subsequent thoughts and behaviours? In a landmark study, had participants solve a word search puzzle where the answers pertained to words about the elderly (e.g., "old," "grandma") or something random (e.g., "notebook," "tomato"). Afterward, the researchers secretly measured how fast the participants walked down the hallway exiting the experiment. And although none of the participants were aware of a theme to the answers, those who had solved a puzzle with elderly words (vs. those with other types of words) walked more slowly down the hallway!

Text Description automatically generated

This effect is called priming (i.e., readily "activating" certain concepts and associations from one's memory) has been found in a number of other studies. For example, priming people by having them drink from a warm glass (vs. a cold one) resulted in behaving more "warmly" toward others Although all of these influences occur beneath one's conscious awareness, they still have a significant effect on one's subsequent thoughts and behaviours.

In the last two decades, researchers have made advances in studying aspects of psychology that exist beyond conscious awareness. As you can understand, it is difficult to use self-reports and surveys to ask people about motives or beliefs that they, themselves, might not even be aware of! One way of side-stepping this difficulty can be found in the implicit associations test, or IAT This research method uses computers to assess people's reaction times to various stimuli and is a very difficult test to fake because it records automatic reactions that occur in milliseconds. For instance, to shed light on deeply held biases, the IAT might present photographs of European American faces and Asian faces while asking research participants to click buttons indicating either "good" or "bad" as quickly as possible. Even if the participant clicks "good" for every face shown, the IAT can still pick up tiny delays in responding. Delays are associated with more mental effort needed to process information. When information is processed quickly—as in the example of white faces being judged as "good"—it can be contrasted with slower processing—as in the example of Asian faces being judged as "good"—and the difference in processing speed is reflective of bias. In this regard, the IAT has been used for investigating stereotypes as well as self-esteem. This method can help uncover non-conscious biases as well as those that we are motivated to suppress.

An actual screenshot from an IAT (Implicit Association Test) that a person might take to test their own mental representations of various cognitive constructs. In this case, this is an item testing an individual's unconscious reaction towards members of various ethnic groups. [Image: Courtesy of Anthony Greenwald from Project Implicit]

High Awareness

Just because we may be influenced by these "invisible" factors, it doesn't mean we are helplessly controlled by them. The other side of the awareness continuum is known as "high awareness." This includes effortful attention and careful decision making. For example, when you listen to a funny story on a date, or consider which class schedule would be preferable, or complete a complex math problem, you are engaging a state of consciousness that allows you to be highly aware of and focused on particular details in your environment.

A young man sits in the lotus position meditating.

Meditation has been practiced for centuries in religious contexts. In the past 50 years it has become increasingly popular as a secular practice. Scientific studies have linked meditation to lower stress and higher well-being.

Mindfulness is a state of higher consciousness that includes an awareness of the thoughts passing through one's head. For example, have you ever snapped at someone in frustration, only to take a moment and reflect on why you responded so aggressively? This more effortful consideration of your thoughts could be described as an expansion of your conscious awareness as you take the time to consider the possible influences on your thoughts. Research has shown that when you engage in this more deliberate consideration, you are less persuaded by irrelevant yet biasing influences, like the presence of a celebrity in an advertisement. Higher awareness is also associated with recognizing when you're using a stereotype, rather than fairly evaluating another person Humans alternate between low and high thinking states. That is, we shift between focused attention and a less attentive default sate, and we have neural networks for both. Interestingly, the the less we're paying attention, the more likely we are to be influenced by non-conscious stimuli (Although these subtle influences may affect us, we can use our higher conscious awareness to protect against external influences. In what's known as the <u>Flexible Correction Model</u> (people who are aware that their thoughts or behaviour are being influenced by an undue, outside source, can correct their attitude against the bias. For example, you might be aware that you are influenced by mention of specific political parties. If you were motivated to consider a government policy you can take your own biases into account to attempt to consider the policy in a fair way (on its own merits rather than being attached to a certain party).

To help make the relationship between lower and higher consciousness clearer, imagine the brain is like a journey down a river. In low awareness, you simply float on a small rubber raft and let the currents push you. It's not very difficult to just drift along but you also don't have total control. Higher states of consciousness are more like traveling in a canoe. In this scenario, you have a paddle and can steer, but it requires more effort. This analogy applies to many states of consciousness, but not all. What about other states such as like sleeping, daydreaming, or hypnosis? How are these related to our conscious awareness?

A summary of the costs and benefits of high and low awareness as discussed in the text.

Table 1: States of Consciousness

Other States of Consciousness

Hypnosis

If you've ever watched a stage hypnotist perform, it may paint a misleading portrait of this state of consciousness. The hypnotized people on stage, for example, appear to be in a state like sleep. However, as the hypnotist continues with the show, you would recognize some profound differences between sleep and hypnosis. Namely, when you're asleep, hearing the word "strawberry" doesn't make you flap your arms like a chicken. In stage performances, the hypnotized participants appear to be highly suggestible, to the point that they are seemingly under the hypnotist's control. Such performances are entertaining but have a way of sensationalizing the true nature of hypnotic states.

A stage hypnotist holds his hand over the head of a volunteer who falls limp into the arms of the hypnotist's assistant. A group of volunteers seem to be unconscious in their seats in the background.   People

being hypnotized on stage.

Hypnosis is an actual, documented phenomenon—one that has been studied and debated for over 200 years (Franz Mesmer (1734 – 1815) is often credited as among the first people to "discover" hypnosis, which he used to treat members of elite society who were experiencing psychological distress. It is from Mesmer's name that we get the English word, "mesmerize" meaning "to entrance or transfix a person's attention." Mesmer attributed the effect of hypnosis to "animal magnetism," a supposed universal force (like gravity) that operates through all human bodies. Even at the time, such an account of hypnosis was not scientifically supported, and Mesmer himself was frequently the centre of controversy.

Over the years, researchers have proposed that <u>hypnosis</u> is a mental state characterized by reduced peripheral awareness and increased focus on a singular stimulus, which results in an enhanced susceptibility to suggestion. For example, the hypnotist will usually induce hypnosis by getting the person to pay attention only to the hypnotist's voice. As the individual focuses more and more on that, s/he begins to forget the context of the setting and responds to the hypnotist's suggestions as if they were his or her own. Some people are naturally more suggestible, and therefore more "hypnotizable" than are others, and this is especially true for those who score high in empathy .One common "trick" of stage hypnotists is to discard volunteers who are less suggestible than others.

<u>Dissociation</u> is the separation of one's awareness from everything besides what one is centrally focused on. For example, if you've ever been daydreaming in class, you were likely so caught up in the fantasy that you didn't hear a word the teacher said. During hypnosis, this dissociation becomes even more extreme. That is, a person concentrates so much on the words of the hypnotist that s/he loses perspective of the rest of the world around them. Because of dissociation, a person is less effortful, and less self-conscious in consideration of his or her own thoughts and behaviours. Like low awareness states, where one often acts on the first thought that comes to mind, so, too, in hypnosis does the individual simply follow the first thought that comes to mind, i.e., the hypnotist's suggestion. Still, just because one is more susceptible to suggestion under hypnosis, it doesn't mean s/he will do anything that's ordered. To be hypnotized, you must first *want* to be hypnotized (i.e., you can't be hypnotized against your will and once you are hypnotized, you won't do anything you wouldn't also do while in a more natural state of consciousness

Today, <u>hypnotherapy</u> is still used in a variety of formats, and it has evolved from Mesmer's early tinkering with the concept. Modern hypnotherapy often uses a combination of relaxation, suggestion, motivation, and expectancies to create a desired mental or behavioural state. Although there is mixed evidence on whether hypnotherapy can help with addiction reduction) there is some evidence that it can be successful in treating sufferers of acute and chronic pain. For example, one study examined the treatment of burn patients with either hypnotherapy, pseudo-hypnosis (i.e., a placebo condition), or no treatment at all. Afterward, even though people in the placebo condition experienced a 16% decrease in pain, those in the actual hypnosis condition experienced a reduction of nearly 50%. Thus, even though hypnosis may be sensationalized for television and movies, its ability to disassociate a person from their environment (or their pain) in conjunction with increased suggestibility to a clinician's recommendations (e.g., "you will feel less anxiety about your chronic pain") is a documented practice with actual medical benefits.

Now, similar to hypnotic states, <u>trance states</u> also involve a dissociation of the self; however, people in a trance state are said to have less voluntary control over their behaviours and actions. Trance states often occur in religious ceremonies, where the person believes he or she is "possessed" by an otherworldly being or force. While in trance, people report anecdotal accounts of a "higher consciousness" or communion with a greater power. However, the body of research investigating this phenomenon tends to reject the claim that these experiences constitute an "altered state of consciousness."

Most researchers today describe both hypnosis and trance states as "subjective" alterations of consciousness, not a distinct or evolved form. Just like you feel different when you're in a state of deep relaxation, so, too, are hypnotic and trance states simply shifts from the standard conscious experience. Researchers contend that even though both hypnotic and trance states appear and feel wildly different than the normal human experience, they can be explained by standard socio-cognitive factors like imagination, expectation, and the interpretation of the situation.

Sleep

A man dressed in pajamas sits up in bed as he stretches and yawns.   Sleep is
necessary for people to function well.

You may have experienced the sensation-- as you are falling asleep-- of falling and then found yourself physically jerking forward and grabbing out as if you were really falling. Sleep is a unique state of consciousness; it lacks full awareness, but the brain is still active. People generally follow a "biological clock" that impacts when they naturally become drowsy, when they fall asleep, and the time they naturally awaken. The hormone melatonin increases at night and is associated with becoming sleepy. Your natural daily rhythm, or Circadian Rhythm, can be influenced by the amount of daylight to which you are exposed as well as your work and activity schedule. Changing your location, such as flying from Canada to England, can disrupt your natural sleep rhythms, and we call this jet lag. You can overcome jet lag by synchronizing yourself to the local schedule by exposing yourself to daylight and forcing yourself to stay awake even though you are naturally sleepy.

Interestingly, sleep itself is more than shutting off for the night (or for a nap). Instead of turning off like a light with a flick of a switch, your shift in consciousness is reflected in your brain's electrical activity. While you are awake and alert your brain, activity is marked by *beta* waves. Beta waves are characterized by being high in frequency but low in intensity. In addition, they are the most inconsistent brain wave, and this reflects the wide variation in sensory input that a person processes during the day. As you begin to relax these changes to *alpha* waves. These waves reflect brain activity that is less frequent, more consistent, and more intense. As you slip into actual sleep you transition through many stages. Scholars differ on how they characterize sleep stages with some experts arguing that there are four distinct stages while others recognize five but they all distinguish between those that include rapid eye movement (REM) and those that are non-rapid eye movement (NREM). In addition, each stage is typically characterized by its own unique pattern of brain activity:

- Stage 1 (called NREM 1, or N1) is the "falling asleep" stage and is marked by theta waves.
- Stage 2 (called NREM 2, or N2) is considered a light sleep. Here, there are occasional "sleep spindles," or very high intensity brain waves. These are thought to be associated with the processing of memories. NREM 2 makes up about 55% of all sleep.
- Stage 3 (called NREM 3, or N3) makes up between 20-25% of all sleep and is marked by greater muscle relaxation and the appearance of delta waves.
- Finally, REM sleep is marked by rapid eye movement (REM). Interestingly, this stage—in terms of brain activity—is like wakefulness. That is, the brain waves occur less intensely than in other stages of sleep. REM sleep accounts for about 20% of all sleep and is associated with dreaming.

Image accompanies the previously listed stages of sleep Figure 1.

Changes in brain activity or brainwaves across different stages of consciousness – from being awake and throughout various stages of sleep. Dreams are, arguably, the most interesting aspect of sleep. Throughout history dreams have been given special importance because of their unique, almost mystical nature. They have been thought to be predictions of the future, hints of hidden aspects of the self, important lessons about how to live life, or opportunities to engage in impossible deeds like flying. There are several competing theories of why humans dream. One is that it is our nonconscious attempt to make sense of our daily experiences and learning. Another, popularized by Freud, is that dreams represent taboo or troublesome wishes or desires. Regardless of the specific reason we know a few facts about dreams: all humans dream, we dream at every stage of sleep, but dreams during REM sleep are especially vivid. One under-explored area of dream research is the possible social functions of dreams: we often share our dreams with others and use them for entertainment value.

Sleep serves many functions, one of which is to give us a period of mental and physical restoration. Children generally need more sleep than adults since they are developing. It is so vital, in fact, that a lack of sleep is associated with a wide range of problems. People who do not receive adequate sleep are more irritable, have slower reaction time, have more difficulty sustaining attention, and make poorer decisions. Interestingly, this is an issue relevant to the lives of college students. In one highly cited study researchers found that 1 in 5 students took more than 30 minutes to fall asleep at night, 1 in 10 occasionally took sleep medications, and more than half reported being "mostly tired" in the mornings.

Psychoactive Drugs

On April 16, 1943, Albert Hoffman—a Swiss chemist working in a pharmaceutical company—accidentally ingested a newly synthesized drug. The drug—lysergic acid diethylamide (LSD)—turned out to be a powerful hallucinogen. Hoffman went home and later reported the effects of the drug, describing them as seeing the world through a "warped mirror" and experiencing visions of "extraordinary shapes with intense, kaleidoscopic play of colours." Hoffman had discovered what members of many traditional cultures around the world already knew: there are substances that, when ingested, can have a powerful effect on perception and on consciousness.

Drugs operate on human physiology in a variety of ways and researchers and medical doctors tend to classify drugs according to their effects. Here we will briefly cover 3 categories of drugs: hallucinogens, depressants, and stimulants.

Hallucinogens

It is possible that hallucinogens are the substance that have, historically, been used the most widely. Traditional societies have used plant-based hallucinogens such as peyote, been, and psilocybin mushrooms in a wide range of religious ceremonies. <u>Hallucinogens</u> are substances that alter a person's perceptions, often by creating visions or hallucinations that are not real. There are a wide range of hallucinogens and many are used as recreational substances in industrialized societies. Common examples include marijuana, LSD, and MDMA (also known as "ecstasy"). Marijuana is the dried flowers of the hemp plant and is often smoked to produce <u>euphoria</u>. The active ingredient in marijuana is called THC and can produce distortions in the perception of time, can create a sense of rambling, unrelated thoughts, and is sometimes associated with increased hunger or excessive laughter. The use and possession of marijuana is illegal in most places, but this appears to be a trend that is changing. Uruguay, Bangladesh, and several of the United States, have recently legalized marijuana. This may be due, in part, to changing public attitudes or to the fact that marijuana is increasingly used for medical purposes such as the management of nausea or treating glaucoma.

Depressants

<u>Depressants</u> are substances that, as their name suggests, slow down the body's physiology and mental processes. Alcohol is the most widely used depressant. Alcohol's effects include the reduction of inhibition, meaning that intoxicated people are more likely to act in ways they would otherwise be reluctant to. Alcohol's psychological effects are the result of it increasing the neurotransmitter GABA. There are also physical effects, such as loss of balance and coordination, and these stem from the way that alcohol interferes with the coordination of the visual and motor systems of the brain. Even though alcohol is so widely accepted in many cultures it is also associated with a variety of dangers. First, alcohol is toxic, meaning that it acts like a poison because it is possible to drink more alcohol than the body can effectively remove from the bloodstream. When a person's <u>blood alcohol content (BAC)</u> reaches .3 to .4% there is a serious risk of death. Second, the lack of judgment and physical control associated with alcohol is associated with more risk-taking behaviour or dangerous behaviour such as drunk driving. Finally, alcohol is addictive and heavy drinkers often experience significant interference with their ability to work effectively or in their close relationships.

Other common depressants include opiates (also called "narcotics"), which are substances synthesized from the poppy flower. Opiates stimulate endorphin production in the brain and because of this they are often used as pain killers by medical professionals. Unfortunately, because opiates such as Oxycontin so reliably produce euphoria they are increasingly used—illegally—as recreational substances. Opiates are highly addictive.

Stimulants

A cup of black coffee.

Caffeine is the most widely consumed stimulant in the world. Be honest, how many cups of coffee, tea, or energy drinks have you had today?

Stimulants are substances that "speed up" the body's physiological and mental processes. Two commonly used stimulants are caffeine—the drug found in coffee and tea—and nicotine, the active drug in cigarettes and other tobacco products. These substances are both legal and relatively inexpensive, leading to their widespread use. Many people are attracted to stimulants because they feel more alert when under the influence of these drugs. As with any drug there are health risks associated with consumption. For example, excessive consumption of these types of stimulants can result in anxiety, headaches, and insomnia. Similarly, smoking cigarettes—the most common means of ingesting nicotine—is associated with higher risks of cancer. For instance, among heavy smokers 90% of lung cancer is directly attributable to smoking

There are other stimulants such as cocaine and methamphetamine (also known as "crystal meth" or "ice") that are illegal substances that are commonly used. These substances act by blocking "re-uptake" of dopamine in the brain. This means that the brain does not naturally clear out the dopamine and that it builds up in the synapse, creating euphoria and alertness. As the effects wear off it stimulates strong cravings for more of the drug. Because of this these powerful stimulants are highly addictive.

Conclusion

When you think about your daily life it is easy to get lulled into the belief that there is one "setting" for your conscious thought. That is, you likely believe that you hold the same opinions, values, and memories across the day and throughout the week. But "you" are like a dimmer switch on a light that can be turned from full darkness increasingly on up to full brightness. This switch is consciousness. At your brightest setting you are fully alert and aware; at dimmer settings you are daydreaming; and sleep or being knocked unconscious represent dimmer settings still. The degree to which you are in high, medium, or low states of conscious awareness affect how susceptible you are to persuasion, how clear your judgment is, and how much detail you can recall. Understanding levels of awareness, then, is at the heart of understanding how we learn, decide, remember and many other vital psychological processes.

THE END

This guy is singing his heart out in his one-man mobile music studio. Have you ever done this?

Consciousness is a term meant to indicate awareness. It includes awareness of the self, of bodily sensations, of thoughts and of the environment. In English, we use the opposite word "unconscious" to indicate senselessness or a barrier to awareness, as in the case of "Theresa fell off the ladder and hit her head, knocking herself unconscious." And yet, psychological theory and research suggest that consciousness and unconsciousness are more complicated than falling off a ladder. That is, consciousness is more than just being "on" or "off." For instance, Sigmund Freud (1856 – 1939)—a psychological theorist—understood that even while we are awake, many things lay outside the realm of our conscious awareness (like being in the car and forgetting the rest of the world can see into your windows). In response to this notion, Freud introduced the concept of the "subconscious" and proposed that some of our memories and even our basic motivations are not always accessible to our conscious minds.

Upon reflection, it is easy to see how slippery a topic consciousness is. For example, are people conscious when they are daydreaming? What about when they are drunk? In this module, we will describe several levels of consciousness and then discuss altered states of consciousness such as hypnosis and sleep.

Levels of Awareness

In 1957, a marketing researcher inserted the words "Eat Popcorn" onto one frame of a film being shown across the United States. And although that frame was only projected onto the movie screen for 1/24th of a second—a speed too fast to be perceived by conscious awareness—the researcher reported an increase in popcorn sales by nearly 60%. Almost immediately, all forms of "subliminal messaging" were regulated in the US and banned in countries such as Australia and the United Kingdom. Even though it was later shown that the researcher had made up the data (he hadn't even inserted the words into the film), this fear about influences on our subconscious persists. At its heart, this issue pits various levels of awareness against one another. On the one hand, we have the "low awareness" of subtle, even subliminal influences. On the other hand, there is you—the conscious thinking, feeling you, which includes all that you are currently aware of, even reading this sentence. However, when we consider these different levels of awareness separately, we can better understand how they operate.

Low Awareness

You are constantly receiving and evaluating sensory information. Although each moment has too many sights, smells, and sounds for them all to be consciously considered, our brains are nonetheless processing all that information. For example, have you ever been at a party, overwhelmed by all the people and conversation, when out of nowhere you hear your name called? Even though you have no idea what else the person is saying, you are somehow conscious of your name (for more on this, "the cocktail party effect," see Nobu's Module on Attention). So, even though you may not be aware of various stimuli in your environment, your brain is paying closer attention than you think.

Similar to a reflex (like jumping when startled), some cues, or significant sensory information, will automatically elicit a response from us even though we never consciously perceive it. For example, Lohman and Soares measured subtle variations in sweating of participants with a fear of snakes. The researchers flashed pictures of different objects (e.g., mushrooms, flowers, and most importantly, snakes) on a screen in front of them, but did so at speeds that left the participant clueless as to what he or she had actually seen. However, when snake pictures were flashed, these participants started sweating more (i.e., a sign of fear), even though they had no idea what they'd just viewed!

Although our brains perceive some stimuli without our conscious awareness, do they really affect our subsequent thoughts and behaviours? In a landmark study, had participants solve a word search puzzle where the answers pertained to words about the elderly (e.g., "old," "grandma") or something random (e.g., "notebook," "tomato"). Afterward, the researchers secretly measured how fast the participants walked down the hallway exiting the experiment. And although none of the participants were aware of a theme to the answers, those who had solved a puzzle with elderly words (vs. those with other types of words) walked more slowly down the hallway!

Text Description automatically generated

This effect is called priming (i.e., readily "activating" certain concepts and associations from one's memory) has been found in a number of other studies. For example, priming people by having them drink from a warm glass (vs. a cold one) resulted in behaving more "warmly" toward others Although all of these influences occur beneath one's conscious awareness, they still have a significant effect on one's subsequent thoughts and behaviours.

In the last two decades, researchers have made advances in studying aspects of psychology that exist beyond conscious awareness. As you can understand, it is difficult to use self-reports and surveys to ask people about motives or beliefs that they, themselves, might not even be aware of! One way of side-stepping this difficulty can be found in the <u>implicit associations test</u>, or IAT This research method uses computers to assess people's reaction times to various stimuli and is a very difficult test to fake because it records automatic reactions that occur in milliseconds. For instance, to shed light on deeply held biases, the IAT might present photographs of European American faces and Asian faces while asking research participants to click buttons indicating either "good" or "bad" as quickly as possible. Even if the participant clicks "good" for every face shown, the IAT can still pick up tiny delays in responding. Delays are associated with more mental effort needed to process information. When information is processed quickly—as in the example of white faces being judged as "good"—it can be contrasted with slower processing—as in the example of Asian faces being judged as "good"—and the difference in processing speed is reflective of bias. In this regard, the IAT has been used for investigating stereotypes as well as self-esteem. This method can help uncover non-conscious biases as well as those that we are motivated to suppress.

An actual screenshot from an IAT (Implicit Association Test) that a person might take to test their own mental representations of various cognitive constructs. In this case, this is an item testing an individual's unconscious reaction towards members of various ethnic groups. [Image: Courtesy of Anthony Greenwald from Project Implicit]

High Awareness

Just because we may be influenced by these "invisible" factors, it doesn't mean we are helplessly controlled by them. The other side of the awareness continuum is known as "high awareness." This includes effortful attention and careful decision making. For example, when you listen to a funny story on a date, or consider which class schedule would be preferable, or complete a complex math problem, you are engaging a state of consciousness that allows you to be highly aware of and focused on particular details in your environment.

A young man sits in the lotus position meditating.

Meditation has been practiced for centuries in religious contexts. In the past 50 years it has become increasingly popular as a secular practice. Scientific studies have linked meditation to lower stress and higher well-being.

Mindfulness is a state of higher consciousness that includes an awareness of the thoughts passing through one's head. For example, have you ever snapped at someone in frustration, only to take a moment and reflect on why you responded so aggressively? This more effortful consideration of your thoughts could be described as an expansion of your conscious awareness as you take the time to consider the possible influences on your thoughts. Research has shown that when you engage in this more deliberate consideration, you are less persuaded by irrelevant yet biasing influences, like the presence of a celebrity in an advertisement. Higher awareness is also associated with recognizing when you're using a stereotype, rather than fairly evaluating another person Humans alternate between low and high thinking states. That is, we shift between focused attention and a less attentive default sate, and we have neural networks for both. Interestingly, the the less we're paying attention, the more likely we are to be influenced by non-conscious stimuli (Although these subtle influences may affect us, we can use our higher conscious awareness to protect against external influences. In what's known as the Flexible Correction Model (people who are aware that their thoughts or behaviour are being influenced by an undue, outside source, can correct their attitude against the bias. For example, you might be aware that you are influenced by mention of specific political parties. If you were motivated to consider a government policy you can take your own biases into account to attempt to consider the policy in a fair way (on its own merits rather than being attached to a certain party).

To help make the relationship between lower and higher consciousness clearer, imagine the brain is like a journey down a river. In low awareness, you simply float on a small rubber raft and let the currents push you. It's not very difficult to just drift along but you also don't have total control. Higher states of consciousness are more like traveling in a canoe. In this scenario, you have a paddle and can steer, but it requires more effort. This analogy applies to many states of consciousness, but not all. What about other states such as like sleeping, daydreaming, or hypnosis? How are these related to our conscious awareness?

A summary of the costs and benefits of high and low awareness as discussed in the text.

Table 1: States of Consciousness

Other States of Consciousness

Hypnosis

If you've ever watched a stage hypnotist perform, it may paint a misleading portrait of this state of consciousness. The hypnotized people on stage, for example, appear to be in a state like sleep. However, as the hypnotist continues with the show, you would recognize some profound differences between sleep and hypnosis. Namely, when you're asleep, hearing the word "strawberry" doesn't make you flap your arms like a chicken. In stage performances, the hypnotized participants appear to be highly suggestible, to the point that they are seemingly under the hypnotist's control. Such performances are entertaining but have a way of sensationalizing the true nature of hypnotic states.

A stage hypnotist holds his hand over the head of a volunteer who falls limp into the arms of the hypnotist's assistant. A group of volunteers seem to be unconscious in their seats in the background.   People

being hypnotized on stage.

Hypnosis is an actual, documented phenomenon—one that has been studied and debated for over 200 years (Franz Mesmer (1734 – 1815) is often credited as among the first people to "discover" hypnosis, which he used to treat members of elite society who were experiencing psychological distress. It is from Mesmer's name that we get the English word, "mesmerize" meaning "to entrance or transfix a person's attention." Mesmer attributed the effect of hypnosis to "animal magnetism," a supposed universal force (like gravity) that operates through all human bodies. Even at the time, such an account of hypnosis was not scientifically supported, and Mesmer himself was frequently the centre of controversy.

Over the years, researchers have proposed that <u>hypnosis</u> is a mental state characterized by reduced peripheral awareness and increased focus on a singular stimulus, which results in an enhanced susceptibility to suggestion. For example, the hypnotist will usually induce hypnosis by getting the person to pay attention only to the hypnotist's voice. As the individual focuses more and more on that, s/he begins to forget the context of the setting and responds to the hypnotist's suggestions as if they were his or her own. Some people are naturally more suggestible, and therefore more "hypnotizable" than are others, and this is especially true for those who score high in empathy .One common "trick" of stage hypnotists is to discard volunteers who are less suggestible than others.

<u>Dissociation</u> is the separation of one's awareness from everything besides what one is centrally focused on. For example, if you've ever been daydreaming in class, you were likely so caught up in the fantasy that you didn't hear a word the teacher said. During hypnosis, this dissociation becomes even more extreme. That is, a person concentrates so much on the words of the hypnotist that s/he loses perspective of the rest of the world around them. Because of dissociation, a person is less effortful, and less self-conscious in consideration of his or her own thoughts and behaviours. Like low awareness states, where one often acts on the first thought that comes to mind, so, too, in hypnosis does the individual simply follow the first thought that comes to mind, i.e., the hypnotist's suggestion. Still, just because one is more susceptible to suggestion under hypnosis, it doesn't mean s/he will do anything that's ordered. To be hypnotized, you must first *want* to be hypnotized (i.e., you can't be hypnotized against your will and once you are hypnotized, you won't do anything you wouldn't also do while in a more natural state of consciousness

Today, <u>hypnotherapy</u> is still used in a variety of formats, and it has evolved from Mesmer's early tinkering with the concept. Modern hypnotherapy often uses a combination of relaxation, suggestion, motivation, and expectancies to create a desired mental or behavioural state. Although there is mixed evidence on whether hypnotherapy can help with addiction reduction) there is some evidence that it can be successful in treating sufferers of acute and chronic pain. For example, one study examined the treatment of burn patients with either hypnotherapy, pseudo-hypnosis (i.e., a placebo condition), or no treatment at all. Afterward, even though people in the placebo condition experienced a 16% decrease in pain, those in the actual hypnosis condition experienced a reduction of nearly 50%. Thus, even though hypnosis may be sensationalized for television and movies, its ability to disassociate a person from their environment (or their pain) in conjunction with increased suggestibility to a clinician's recommendations (e.g., "you will feel less anxiety about your chronic pain") is a documented practice with actual medical benefits.

Now, similar to hypnotic states, <u>trance states</u> also involve a dissociation of the self; however, people in a trance state are said to have less voluntary control over their behaviours and actions. Trance states often occur in religious ceremonies, where the person believes he or she is "possessed" by an otherworldly being or force. While in trance, people report anecdotal accounts of a "higher consciousness" or communion with a greater power. However, the body of research investigating this phenomenon tends to reject the claim that these experiences constitute an "altered state of consciousness."

Most researchers today describe both hypnosis and trance states as "subjective" alterations of consciousness, not a distinct or evolved form. Just like you feel different when you're in a state of deep relaxation, so, too, are hypnotic and trance states simply shifts from the standard conscious experience. Researchers contend that even though both hypnotic and trance states appear and feel wildly different than the normal human experience, they can be explained by standard socio-cognitive factors like imagination, expectation, and the interpretation of the situation.

Sleep

A man dressed in pajamas sits up in bed as he stretches and yawns.   Sleep is

necessary for people to function well.

You may have experienced the sensation-- as you are falling asleep-- of falling and then found yourself physically jerking forward and grabbing out as if you were really falling. Sleep is a unique state of consciousness; it lacks full awareness, but the brain is still active. People generally follow a "biological clock" that impacts when they naturally become drowsy, when they fall asleep, and the time they naturally awaken. The hormone melatonin increases at night and is associated with becoming sleepy. Your natural daily rhythm, or Circadian Rhythm, can be influenced by the amount of daylight to which you are exposed as well as your work and activity schedule. Changing your location, such as flying from Canada to England, can disrupt your natural sleep rhythms, and we call this jet lag. You can overcome jet lag by synchronizing yourself to the local schedule by exposing yourself to daylight and forcing yourself to stay awake even though you are naturally sleepy.

Interestingly, sleep itself is more than shutting off for the night (or for a nap). Instead of turning off like a light with a flick of a switch, your shift in consciousness is reflected in your brain's electrical activity. While you are awake and alert your brain, activity is marked by *beta* waves. Beta waves are characterized by being high in frequency but low in intensity. In addition, they are the most inconsistent brain wave, and this reflects the wide variation in sensory input that a person processes during the day. As you begin to relax these changes to *alpha* waves. These waves reflect brain activity that is less frequent, more consistent, and more intense. As you slip into actual sleep you transition through many stages. Scholars differ on how they characterize sleep stages with some experts arguing that there are four distinct stages while others recognize five but they all distinguish between those that include rapid eye movement (REM) and those that are non-rapid eye movement (NREM). In addition, each stage is typically characterized by its own unique pattern of brain activity:

- Stage 1 (called NREM 1, or N1) is the "falling asleep" stage and is marked by theta waves.
- Stage 2 (called NREM 2, or N2) is considered a light sleep. Here, there are occasional "sleep spindles," or very high intensity brain waves. These are thought to be associated with the processing of memories. NREM 2 makes up about 55% of all sleep.
- Stage 3 (called NREM 3, or N3) makes up between 20-25% of all sleep and is marked by greater muscle relaxation and the appearance of delta waves.
- Finally, REM sleep is marked by rapid eye movement (REM). Interestingly, this stage—in terms of brain activity—is like wakefulness. That is, the brain waves occur less intensely than in other stages of sleep. REM sleep accounts for about 20% of all sleep and is associated with dreaming.

Image accompanies the previously listed stages of sleep Figure 1.

Changes in brain activity or brainwaves across different stages of consciousness – from being awake and throughout various stages of sleep. Dreams are, arguably, the most interesting aspect of sleep. Throughout history dreams have been given special importance because of their unique, almost mystical nature. They have been thought to be predictions of the future, hints of hidden aspects of the self, important lessons about how to live life, or opportunities to engage in impossible deeds like flying. There are several competing theories of why humans dream. One is that it is our nonconscious attempt to make sense of our daily experiences and learning. Another, popularized by Freud, is that dreams represent taboo or troublesome wishes or desires. Regardless of the specific reason we know a few facts about dreams: all humans dream, we dream at every stage of sleep, but dreams during REM sleep are especially vivid. One under-explored area of dream research is the possible social functions of dreams: we often share our dreams with others and use them for entertainment value.

Sleep serves many functions, one of which is to give us a period of mental and physical restoration. Children generally need more sleep than adults since they are developing. It is so vital, in fact, that a lack of sleep is associated with a wide range of problems. People who do not receive adequate sleep are more irritable, have slower reaction time, have more difficulty sustaining attention, and make poorer decisions. Interestingly, this is an issue relevant to the lives of college students. In one highly cited study researchers found that 1 in 5 students took more than 30 minutes to fall asleep at night, 1 in 10 occasionally took sleep medications, and more than half reported being "mostly tired" in the mornings.

Psychoactive Drugs

On April 16, 1943, Albert Hoffman—a Swiss chemist working in a pharmaceutical company—accidentally ingested a newly synthesized drug. The drug—lysergic acid diethylamide (LSD)—turned out to be a powerful hallucinogen. Hoffman went home and later reported the effects of the drug, describing them as seeing the world through a "warped mirror" and experiencing visions of "extraordinary shapes with intense, kaleidoscopic play of colours." Hoffman had discovered what members of many traditional cultures around the world already knew: there are substances that, when ingested, can have a powerful effect on perception and on consciousness.

Drugs operate on human physiology in a variety of ways and researchers and medical doctors tend to classify drugs according to their effects. Here we will briefly cover 3 categories of drugs: hallucinogens, depressants, and stimulants.

Hallucinogens

It is possible that hallucinogens are the substance that have, historically, been used the most widely. Traditional societies have used plant-based hallucinogens such as peyote, been, and psilocybin mushrooms in a wide range of religious ceremonies. <u>Hallucinogens</u> are substances that alter a person's perceptions, often by creating visions or hallucinations that are not real. There are a wide range of hallucinogens and many are used as recreational substances in industrialized societies. Common examples include marijuana, LSD, and MDMA (also known as "ecstasy"). Marijuana is the dried flowers of the hemp plant and is often smoked to produce <u>euphoria</u>. The active ingredient in marijuana is called THC and can produce distortions in the perception of time, can create a sense of rambling, unrelated thoughts, and is sometimes associated with increased hunger or excessive laughter. The use and possession of marijuana is illegal in most places, but this appears to be a trend that is changing. Uruguay, Bangladesh, and several of the United States, have recently legalized marijuana. This may be due, in part, to changing public attitudes or to the fact that marijuana is increasingly used for medical purposes such as the management of nausea or treating glaucoma.

Depressants

<u>Depressants</u> are substances that, as their name suggests, slow down the body's physiology and mental processes. Alcohol is the most widely used depressant. Alcohol's effects include the reduction of inhibition, meaning that intoxicated people are more likely to act in ways they would otherwise be reluctant to. Alcohol's psychological effects are the result of it increasing the neurotransmitter GABA. There are also physical effects, such as loss of balance and coordination, and these stem from the way that alcohol interferes with the coordination of the visual and motor systems of the brain. Even though alcohol is so widely accepted in many cultures it is also associated with a variety of dangers. First, alcohol is toxic, meaning that it acts like a poison because it is possible to drink more alcohol than the body can effectively remove from the bloodstream. When a person's <u>blood alcohol content (BAC)</u> reaches .3 to .4% there is a serious risk of death. Second, the lack of judgment and physical control associated with alcohol is associated with more risk-taking behaviour or dangerous behaviour such as drunk driving. Finally, alcohol is addictive and heavy drinkers often experience significant interference with their ability to work effectively or in their close relationships.

Other common depressants include opiates (also called "narcotics"), which are substances synthesized from the poppy flower. Opiates stimulate endorphin production in the brain and because of this they are often used as pain killers by medical professionals. Unfortunately, because opiates such as Oxycontin so reliably produce euphoria they are increasingly used—illegally—as recreational substances. Opiates are highly addictive.

Stimulants

A cup of black coffee.   Caffeine is the most widely

consumed stimulant in the world. Be honest, how many cups of coffee, tea, or energy drinks have you had today?

Stimulants are substances that "speed up" the body's physiological and mental processes. Two commonly used stimulants are caffeine—the drug found in coffee and tea—and nicotine, the active drug in cigarettes and other tobacco products. These substances are both legal and relatively inexpensive, leading to their widespread use. Many people are attracted to stimulants because they feel more alert when under the influence of these drugs. As with any drug there are health risks associated with consumption. For example, excessive consumption of these types of stimulants can result in anxiety, headaches, and insomnia. Similarly, smoking cigarettes—the most common means of ingesting nicotine—is associated with higher risks of cancer. For instance, among heavy smokers 90% of lung cancer is directly attributable to smoking

There are other stimulants such as cocaine and methamphetamine (also known as "crystal meth" or "ice") that are illegal substances that are commonly used. These substances act by blocking "re-uptake" of dopamine in the brain. This means that the brain does not naturally clear out the dopamine and that it builds up in the synapse, creating euphoria and alertness. As the effects wear off it stimulates strong cravings for more of the drug. Because of this these powerful stimulants are highly addictive.

Conclusion

When you think about your daily life it is easy to get lulled into the belief that there is one "setting" for your conscious thought. That is, you likely believe that you hold the same opinions, values, and memories across the day and throughout the week. But "you" are like a dimmer switch on a light that can be turned from full darkness increasingly on up to full brightness. This switch is consciousness. At your brightest setting you are fully alert and aware; at dimmer settings you are daydreaming; and sleep or being knocked unconscious represent dimmer settings still. The degree to which you are in high, medium, or low states of conscious awareness affect how susceptible you are to persuasion, how clear your judgment is, and how much detail you can recall. Understanding levels of awareness, then, is at the heart of understanding how we learn, decide, remember and many other vital psychological processes.

THE END

Contents